D1453287

DEPENDENT DEVELOPMENT AND INDUSTRIAL ORDER

DEPENDENT DEVELOPMENT AND INDUSTRIAL ORDER

An Asian Case Study

Frederic C. Deyo

PRAEGER

PRAEGER SPECIAL STUDIES • PRAEGER SCIENTIFIC

Library of Congress Cataloging in Publication Data

Deyo, Frederic C
  Dependent development and industrial order.

  Bibliography: p.
  Includes index.
  1. Singapore--Industries. 2. Industrial re-
lations--Singapore. 3. Investments, Foreign--
Singapore. 4. Underdeveloped areas--Industries--
Case studies. 5. Underdeveloped areas--Industrial
relations--Case studies. 6. Underdeveloped areas--
Investments, Foreign--Case studies. I. Title.
HC445.8.D49 1981   338.09595'7   80-22873
ISBN 0-03-047386-1

Published in 1981 by Praeger Publishers
CBS Educational and Professional Publishing
A Division of CBS, Inc.
521 Fifth Avenue, New York, New York 10175 U.S.A.

© 1981 by Praeger Publishers

123456789   145   987654321

Printed in the United States of America

In memory of my father.

ACKNOWLEDGMENTS

I wish to thank my friends and former colleagues at the University of Singapore for their patience and indulgence in helping me to come to terms, both intellectually and emotionally, with the political and moral realities of Singapore. I also thank Janet Salaff, Robert Snow, and Aline Wong for their very helpful criticism of an earlier draft of the manuscript, as well as Lou Zicari for his tireless research assistance. My greatest debt, however, goes to my wife, Judy, and our three children, Raymond, Diana, and Peter, who sacrificed the most for "Daddy's Book."

CONTENTS

LIST OF TABLES

LIST OF FIGURE

INTRODUCTION

There can be little question that industrialization in western countries was associated with painful periods of social dislocation for many occupational groups (Wilensky 1958). Especially well documented were the exploitation and social and cultural marginalization of industrial workers in growing factory towns (Polanyi 1944). But equally clear, too, was the subsequent evolution of new social forms and cultural values which reintegrated labor into an emerging industrial society. And, above all else, trade unions provided an indispensable basis for such integration.

Industrialization in the third world today has created many of the same problems of social disorganization encountered in the West. But the unique western politicohistorical context that gave rise not only to economic growth but also to those sociocultural and political changes that provided a basis for a new industrial order is largely lacking in many such countries. To the extent development and order have been achieved, the state has provided the necessary impetus. Such state involvement has in turn often been associated with the imposition of authoritarian corporatist controls over organized labor and the suppression of independent efforts by workers and other affected groups to stake out their own political, social, and economic destinies in the new society. This study examines the relationship between such corporatism on one hand and economic development on the other, in the context of an increasingly common pattern of dependent, world market oriented industrialization.

Third world industrialization efforts are increasingly based on the attraction of foreign investment in export-oriented, labor-intensive manufacturing activities in order to create employment and to gain quick access to international capital, technology, and markets. In many cases, such efforts have included the adoption of authoritarian corporatist labor policies through which to reduce labor costs and conflict as well as to increase labor discipline and productivity. Such policies have in turn encouraged rapid investment and economic growth within foreign economic enclaves comparable in some respects to the earlier enclaves created by foreign-controlled extractive industries. While coercive corporatist controls provide an initial basis for industrial order in these manufacturing enclaves, the subsequent pattern of dualistic economic growth may be associated with growing social disorganization which in turn facilitates an extension and deepening penetration of corporatist controls. However, authoritarian corporatist industrial order engenders a sociopolitical dilemma between the opposed needs for control and demobilization on one hand and institutional commitment and participation on the other. As corporatist controls generate growing industrial morale problems and their attendant economic costs, elites may move toward greater emphasis on popular institutional participation, despite its apparent incompatibility with corporatist structural principles.

This study examines the relationship between corporatist industrial order and dependent world market oriented industrialization as well as institutional adaptations to the corporatist dilemma. Most of the discussion centers on a case study of industrialization in Singapore, a society which provides a relatively "pure" case of the new development strategy.

Chapter 1 presents a general discussion of the literature on authoritarian corporatism in third world industrial relations as well as on the relationship between such corporatism and dependent development. Chapter 2 begins the case study of Singapore with a general description of preindustrial employment relations, while Chapter 3 discusses the emergence of industrial corporatism as a precondition for foreign investment. The following chapter documents the rapid investment inflow beginning in the late 1960s as well as the relative stagnation of domestic private enterprise. Chapters 5 and 6 go on to describe the negative social consequences of authoritarian corporatism and dependent industrialization for local communities and for the social integration of the industrial workforce and also recent state efforts to reinvigorate and refashion the national trade union structure into a more effective instrument not only of workforce discipline but of social integration as well. The final chapter draws out the more general implications of the case study and suggests some longer-term political consequences for this new development pattern.

DEPENDENT DEVELOPMENT AND INDUSTRIAL ORDER

1
LABOR AND STATE IN THIRD WORLD INDUSTRIALIZATION

POLITICAL UNIONISM AND ITS
DEVELOPMENTAL CONSEQUENCES

A striking characteristic of unions in third world countries is
their political orientation: their tendency, that is, to pursue collective goals through political rather than economic means and to be
closely associated with national political parties and elites. Political unionism derives in part from the typically weak economic bargaining position of unions in the context of labor surpluses and economic stagnation, which encourage unions to turn to government for
protection against employers and more generally to pursue bargaining goals through government intervention (Sturmthal 1972; Galenson
1962). Kassalow (1969) has noted that Indian unions have preferred
to retain strong government involvement in disputes settlement
through compulsory arbitration even where there was a possibility
of moving toward more open collective bargaining.

The struggle for independence was itself associated in many
cases with the nationalist mobilization of organized labor to oppose
colonial rule, or with the mobilization of labor support by groups
seeking political and economic transformation and the overthrow of
established antimodernist elites. For example, during the first half
of this century, the middle classes in several Latin American societies mobilized lower-class groups in their effort to overthrow traditional oligarchic elites and introduce new economic policies (Malloy
1977). Such mobilization resulted in a close association of organized
labor with ruling national parties in Argentina, Brazil, and other
countries.

A similar pattern of labor politicization results from competition among aspiring national parties or elites to capture labor support (Kannappan 1968). Such a pattern is especially pronounced in the South Asian countries of Pakistan, India, and Ceylon, where competing political parties have sought to mobilize political support among labor groups. In India, this has been associated with the emergence of several competing labor federations, each aligned with a particular national political party.

Another factor associated with political unionism is the increasing role of government in economic planning and development, a role which encourages unions to address their efforts to public decision-making processes. Closely related to this is the important role of government in industrial relations, a phenomenon with which we shall be centrally concerned in this study. Where government has an important voice in bargaining results, it is government to which unions must turn in their collective efforts to improve wages and work conditions.

The organizational power of unions in third world countries is typically quite minimal. However, the importance of unions in such key economic sectors as transportation, modern industry, and the civil service, in conjunction with the fragility and instability of political regimes in many of these countries, means that politicized unions may either destabilize political regimes (Huntington 1968) or demand economically damaging wage increases, benefits, and welfare expenditures (Johnson 1975).

THE AUTHORITARIAN STATE RESPONSE

If exploitation of labor comprised an important means for capital accumulation and investment in industrializing Europe and the United States, labor organization and politicization prior to industrialization in many third world countries often forces the state to impose political, in lieu of economic, restraints on rising labor costs in order to encourage investment. In particular, elites may attempt to depoliticize labor, stabilize wages and benefits, repress conflict, and establish compulsory disputes settlement machinery (Johnson 1975). This pattern is increasingly common in Latin America, where unions have displayed somewhat greater independence and militance than in Africa and Asia. Starting with the 1964 military coup in Brazil, other countries such as Argentina, Peru, Chile, Uruguay, Bolivia, and Ecuador (Malloy 1977) have produced highly authoritarian, often military-backed, regimes committed to political stabilization and economic growth.

In most cases, such governments have gone beyond the simple suppression of labor organizations to the restructuring of unions and their incorporation into hierarchical networks of dependency vis-a-vis the state. Such "corporatist" systems have been described by Malloy as including:

> strong and relatively autonomous governmental struc-
> tures [which] . . . seek to impose on the society a sys-
> tem of interest representation based on enforced limited
> pluralism. These regimes try to eliminate spontaneous
> interest articulation and establish a limited number of
> authoritatively recognized groups that interact with the
> government apparatus in defined and regularized ways.
> Moreover, the recognized groups in this type of regime
> are organized in vertical, functional categories rather
> than horizontal class categories and are obliged to inter-
> act with the state through the designated leaders of
> authoritatively sanctioned interest associations (p. 4).

Corporatist systems, patterned in part after colonial political structures, are perhaps most highly developed in Brazil, Mexico, and the African Socialist states. They are based on the principle that the interests of the state, as representative of national inter-ests, take precedence over the interests of labor or other special-interest groups (Galenson 1962). In the context of induced moderni-zation, any questioning of national development goals or the policies through which elites pursue them is defined as socially irresponsible and even treasonable. In this sense, corporatism implies a substan-tial depoliticization of popular groups with respect to elite structures and policies.

Corporatism is based on a relationship of economic and politi-cal subordination between the state and particular social groups or classes. Thus, in a given society one may find corporate state-union relations alongside noncorporate relations between the state and religious, business, or other social groups. In some cases, however, corporatism may become so pervasive as to justify refer-ence to a corporatist society. In his discussion of African Socialism, for instance, Friedland (1968) discusses the emergence of "focal in-stitutional societies" in which national ruling parties permeate and control a wide range of social organizations and groups. Suggestive of such a societal model was Nkrumah's reference, in a 1959 speech to an annual delegates' conference of the then ruling Congress People's Party of Ghana, to the nation as a "great tree," the party comprising its roots and trunk, and unions and other social organizations its branches (cited in Friedland 1968).

In corporate systems, unions may be viewed as auxiliaries of ruling parties (Lynd 1968) or as means through which development policies may be implemented. If unions in developed societies often seek "consumptionist" goals of increased wages and benefits for their own members, elites in developing countries may call upon unions to play "productionist" roles supportive of national development (Friedland 1968). In particular, unions are often asked to educate, train, or discipline members; raise productivity; discourage labor-management conflict; restrain wage demands; engage in savings programs; and make whatever other sacrifices are necessary in the national development effort. Following the 1965 corporatist reorganization of Kenya's trade unions under a single, government-controlled labor federation, COTA, President Kenyatta argued that "the first responsibility of the unions must be to develop a disciplined, skilled, and responsible labor force."

In such corporatist systems workers are often viewed primarily as human capital. They are to be recipients of, rather than participants in, policy determination and are dependent on elites and public institutions for moral guidance and secular education (Malloy 1977; Kerr 1960). Collective bargaining, in the context of restrictions on autonomous interest representation, may be partially displaced by government conciliation and arbitration, with economic decisions based less on the relative strengths of opposing sides than on the implications of alternate decisions for development or their conformity to national policy.

SOCIAL FACTORS ASSOCIATED WITH THE
STABILITY OF CORPORATIST SYSTEMS

The long-run stability of corporatism depends in part on a number of conditions that determine the likelihood of effective opposition to state controls. The first and perhaps most important of these conditions is that of a unified political elite. In most cases, this is reflected in the existence of a single dominant political party (Huntington 1968). The oppositional political mobilization of labor is encouraged in situations where there is elite competition, especially where such competition occurs within a multiparty system. Chaplin (1969) has shown, for instance, how Peruvian union politicization was related to the existence of a divided oligarchic elite, while Kearney (1971) has described the politicization of labor in multiparty Ceylon. In both cases, elite competition led to the mobilization of competing labor groups and finally to political instability.

Second, corporatism is strengthened by elite dependence on politically neutral social groups for economic and political resources and by lack of access on the part of potentially oppositional groups to resources over which ruling groups lack control. To the extent ruling elites require the economic support of local business groups for instance or, conversely, where such groups command independent control over important economic resources, they may be in a position to challenge authoritarian rule or to undercut elite autonomy. The pluralism of contemporary European societies derives in part from the rise of a national bourgeoisie which commanded the requisite economic resources to challenge aristocratic elites, just as Latin American oligarchs fell before the revolutionary forces of emerging middle-class groups during the 1930s.

Third, corporatism is based on control over tightly integrated institutional structures and the existence of disorganized nonincorporated sectors, especially where the interests of such nonincorporated sectors are closely affected by government policy and decisions. In the arena of industrial relations, this implies a combination of tightly structured state-affiliated unions within a broader context of workforce and community atomism. Corporatism is most secure where social conditions tend to prevent autonomous interest articulation "through elimination of the conditions which could permit reappearance of demands, leaders, and organization of the popular sector against its political exclusion" (O'Donnell 1977, p. 69). The prevention of autonomous organization and demand formation requires more than just the elimination and suppression of existing nonincorporated labor organizations. Where community structures provide a ready base for oppositional unionism during periods of economic or political uncertainty, latent opposition remains a constant threat to corporatist authority. Argentina's 1968-69 labor radicalization, Pakistan's 1968 political crisis, and Chile's populist revolt of the early 1970s (Kaufman 1977) were all based on the existence of established workers' communities which were able, even under repressive regimes, to maintain independent leadership and organizational bases for oppositional labor movements. In the Argentinian and Chilian cases, this resulted from the development of stable working-class communities during earlier periods of industrialization.

Finally, national elites should control a tightly centralized communications system, centering mainly in the mass media and excluding uncontrolled outside or foreign communications which might introduce oppositional ideologies or challenge established policy.

AUTHORITARIAN CORPORATISM AS INSTITUTIONALIZATION

A corporatist industrialization strategy may be understood in part as a systematic effort on the part of political and economic elites to induce workforce compliance with elite-imposed policies and institutional norms predicated on the requirements of national development and unity. Such a process may be studied at three analytically distinguishable levels of analysis: institutional, cultural, and associational. At the institutional level, one focuses on patterns of norms, rules, laws, and behavioral expectations which regulate and stabilize behavior. The cultural level pertains to abstract values, ideologies, and belief systems which may or may not be consistent with institutional norms and rules. Associational phenomena relate to social affiliations and bonds which draw people together in groups and organizations.

Much of the literature on labor-force commitment to industry in developing societies has dealt with institutional and cultural commitments. Kerr (1964) and Moore (1965), for example, stress the need for newly recruited industrial workers to accept industrial norms of punctuality, work discipline, functional authority, machine pacing, and collective bargaining. Kerr (1964), Dunlop (1958), Moore (1965), and Smelser (1976) have similarly stressed the importance of such ideologies as nationalism, socialism, and religion as sources of legitimation and commitment to industrial norms and rules.

Relatively lacking has been a sustained concern with associational bonds in industrial life or with the relationships between such bonds and institutional or cultural commitments. This overemphasis on institutional and cultural phenomena, which stresses problems of anomie to the neglect of related problems of social atomism, has resulted in an unfortunate and misleading model of labor market behavior which stresses impersonalism, specificity, contractual relations, economic motivation, and lack of affective social bonds (Hoselitz 1973). Such behavior is reflected, presumably, in an individualistic and expedient conformity to industrial norms and sanctions, whether in the context of the unregulated labor market of nineteenth-century England or of a highly state-regulated twentieth-century economy.

An individualistic and atomistic model of labor market behavior and institutional conformity, which, following Moore, may be termed a "pure labor market" model, is neither descriptive of reality nor characteristic of a stable system of employment relations. Belshaw argues in this regard that:

> There is no such thing as an enduring nonpersonalistic relationship, and no economy in the world can be based entirely or even largely on nonpersonalistic relationships, for this would be the negation of continuity and security and would be atomistic group behavior rather than behavior in a society (1965, p. 80).

Similarly, Moore (1951) and Polanyi (1944) have argued that market integration in and of itself would be disruptive and inherently unstable.

More important for our present discussion is Kerr's (1964) contention that atomistic labor market behavior reduces commitment to industrial institutions and norms. It will be argued here that institutional commitments are most stable and reliable when anchored in supportive social bonds relating, in an industrial context, to workgroups, firms, and unions. In this section, we ask the essentially functionalist question: how may such social bonds reinforce (or, conversely, undercut) normative commitments? Later in this discussion, we deal with the more interesting processes through which institutionalization and its associational anchorage emerge.

The relationship between membership in occupational groups and economic associations on one hand and institutional commitment on the other has been noted by Durkheim (1933), Merton (1957), Kerr (1964), and others. In industrial life in particular unions provide economic security that in turn potentially reduces alienation (Kearney 1971) and increases normative commitment (Kerr 1964; Moore 1965), as well as providing a basis for consensus and conformity (Rees 1977).

The importance of associational bonds for institutional commitment stems from several factors. First, association provides a potential basis for socialization, as well as for the internalization of norms (Moore 1965) and of values or ideologies that legitimate those norms (Kearney 1971). Parsons (1951, pp. 193-94) has gone so far as to define institutionalization in part as the internalization of values in need-dispositions. While this extreme position is unnecessary, it may be minimally argued that internalization does reinforce institutional commitment (Etzioni 1964).

Second, association provides the social basis for both formal and informal sanctions by which to reinforce institutional norms. It is well known that strong attachments to firms, workgroups, and unions places them in a strong position to reward and punish behavior as well as to shield individuals from outside countersanctions. The importance of the social control function of groups and associations has been stressed by Parsons who argues that most social control is in fact based on informal sanctions within ongoing social interaction. Similarly, Blau has argued that authority is enhanced by the informal sanctions through which groups of subordinates support compliance with authority. More concretely, the sanction function of associations is seen most clearly in the power of unions to induce membership compliance with contractual provisions of collective agreements (Sufrin 1964).

Associations also facilitate norm adjustment and conflict resolution. This function is most apparent in union-management negotiations, whose success derives in part from the ability of unions to organize membership interests into coherent, bargainable positions vis-a-vis management. In this sense, unions are able to channel protest into socially useful forms (Galenson 1962) and to transform dissent into participation (Huntington 1968) and consensus (Kerr 1964; Dubin 1957).

The general importance of group formation for the organization and institutionalization of conflict has been stressed by Dahrendorf (1959) and Coser (1956), while the more specific relevance of group formation for conflict resolution in third world industrial relations has been discussed by Bates (1970), who argues that unions can provide an important basis for conflict regulation during stressful periods of economic development.

In addition, associations may provide supportive linkages of legitimacy and communication to institutional elites. Unions are especially important as potential support structures for political elites, and thus for the institutional norms such elites may try to impose (Sufrin 1964), while also acting as communication channels between workers and elites. Stalin, for instance, explicitly stressed the role of Soviet unions as "transmission belts" connecting the Communist Party with factory workers.

Finally, it must be stressed that industrial association among workers is double-edged in the sense that it provides the basis for organized and effective opposition as well as support for institutional elites and norms (Kerr and Siegal 1954) and for many of the same reasons already noted with respect to its supportive role. Unions provide an organizational basis for oppositional norms, leadership, and solidarity, just as workgroups can insulate workers from managerial authority. In general, the extent to which association is supportive of institutional elites and norms is determined by the extent to which there is a shared perception that institutional elites are supportive of the interests of rank and file (Seashore 1967), that norms are based on joint determination by elites and nonelites, and that the basic interests of elites are compatible with those of rank and file.

If these comprise some of the conditions under which stable associational bonds may support elite institutional controls, a second question which cannot adequately be addressed here relates to the ways in which associational bonds at levels of workgroup, enterprise, or union are themselves mutually supportive. Because this question will be of some interest later on, a few preliminary observations are useful at this point. First, membership stability in firms with low turnover and absentee rates is supportive of stable workgroup formation as well as of union membership stability where such unions are based on enterprise. Sufrin argues in this regard that union cohesiveness derives in large measure from workplace relations.

Workgroup cohesiveness similarly is supportive of enterprise and union attachments where such groups define these organizational attachments as supportive of group and individual interests and goals. Union solidarity may provide a sense of security and protection for workers, and thus encourage them to remain with given firms even under undesirable conditions, since they have recourse to organized forms of protest in dealing with those conditions. Sharma (1969) found, in his study of Indian factory workers, that union participation rates were strongly correlated with factory attendance. Conversely, close associational affiliations may be mutually incompatible. The workgroup may reinforce negative sentiments toward both the firm and the union, and close personal relations with management may undercut the cohesiveness both of the workgroup and the union, especially in a small, paternalistic firm. We shall return to this problem of mutual reinforcement or antagonism later in the discussion.

AUTHORITARIAN CORPORATISM AND LABOR
FORCE ATOMISM: PROBLEMS OF
ASSOCIATIONAL ANCHORAGE

In societies characterized by corporatist state-labor relations, a number of nonpolitical factors frequently combine with corporatist controls to generate labor force atomism. Such atomism is in turn associated with worker demoralization and lack of commitment to elite-imposed institutional norms relating to enterprise, union, and industrial relations.

It has been noted that bureaucratic-authoritarian corporatism is most stable under conditions of social atomism in spheres of life not effectively brought into the corporatist control structure. But to turn this statement around, political elites may seek to actively demobilize autonomous community and ethnic leadership and organization in order to stabilize corporatist rule. Where such demobilization is effective, industrial workgroups and unions may lack those external solidarities from which to derive group cohesion. Argentinian workers' unions derive strength and support in part from the established worker communities surrounding industrial areas, just as workgroups may form on the basis of shared ethnic or other primordial ties in other societies.

Many characteristics of the industrial workforce in third world countries further reduce the potential for cohesive worker associations or organizational membership stability. The preponderance of poorly educated, low-skilled workers results in a scarcity of potential union leadership and weak occupational identities. In part because of job insecurity, many of these workers are migratory or highly mobile and thus unlikely readily to organize (Sturmthal 1973). And finally, third world labor forces are often marked by far greater ethnocultural heterogeneity than those of European countries (Waterman 1977), in part because of earlier national political demarcation by colonial rulers who ignored natural cultural boundaries. Such heterogeneity hinders the development of occupational interest groups which cut across primordial identities, although these same identities may also provide the basis for cohesive worker associations where they are formed within homogeneous groups.

But probably of greatest importance in determining the strength and significance of workforce associational bonds is the political and industrial structure within which such bonds are formed. Here we shall examine the impact of political corporatist structures for labor force atomism, while in a later section we discuss the relationship between economic structure and worker associations.

Authoritarian corporatist regimes tend to emphasize control at the expense of social and associational mobilization of labor. Such control in part involves the undercutting of several organizational resources of unions, such as the right to strike, the legality of involvement in politics (Kassalow 1969), and the legitimacy of collective bargaining on the basis of group interests. This problem is further exacerbated by the tendency for the state to assume a strong social-welfare role vis-a-vis labor and thus largely to replace the union in matters not only of wage determination but of essential social services as well. The importance and attractiveness of unions to workers is thus reduced by the increasing irrelevance of unions from the standpoint of material welfare.

In addition, the increasing centralization of unions in bureaucratic-authoritarian regimes is associated with a growing gap between workers and union leaders and a resulting decline in psychological involvement and commitment to unions (Friedland 1968). Finally, a unitary corporatist ideology itself undercuts the legitimacy of interest-based associations and their tendency to pursue narrow sectoral goals at the possible expense of national ones (Fox 1971). The net result of such changes is a decline or stagnation in union membership and increasing member apathy (Friedland 1968; Kaufman 1977; O'Donnell 1977).

In general, where authoritarian corporatist regimes have been established, and where the preconditions for the stability of such regimes have been met, the results have been gratifying to political and economic elites. Strikes and industrial conflict have been substantially reduced, political stability enhanced, and investment stimulated. More problematic, however, has been the longer-term effort to capture the loyalty, initiative, and commitment of labor to elite-imposed institutions and policy, at both enterprise and national levels. Friedland notes, for example, the footdragging, lack of worker commitment, and general "reluctance [of workers] to assume a share of the cost of economic development" in African Socialist countries. And Cordova notes that legislative control and suppression of unions in Latin America has tended to encourage "a tendency to anomy, . . . with inevitable disruptive effects on the productive process" (1972, p. 470).

The negative consequences of such institutional demoralization among workers become quickly apparent. In the context of weak worker attachment to government-controlled unions, the capacity of unions effectively to carry out their productionist role in the socialization and discipline of workers is undermined, while workers who lack effective representation continue to engage in such individual forms of worker protest as absenteeism, quitting, and apathetic work performance (Kerr 1964; Kannappan 1968). In both union and enterprise contexts, then, there are increasing manifestations of a lack of associational anchorage for elite-imposed institutional norms relating to employment.

POPULAR-AUTHORITARIAN CORPORATISM: DEPOLITICIZED SOCIAL MOBILIZATION

In several third world countries, governments have reacted to the apparent demoralization and atomization of labor by attempting to reinvigorate government-controlled unions in order better to permit them to play effective productionist roles. In some cases, this has taken the form of mandatory union membership, as in Tanzania (Lynd 1968) and in Ghana under Nkrumah (Friedland 1968). More common is the devolution of important welfare functions to unions (Kerr 1964). In Tanzania, for instance, unions have taken over many formerly state-controlled programs relating to housing, credit unions, and health clinics (Lynd 1968). Similarly, in Kenya COTA is heavily involved in cooperatives, housing, and social security. Additional support of unions may take the form of dues checkoff systems and financial and other assistance from governments.

Such measures, by increasing the economic relevance of unions to workers, have tended to increase rank and file participation and interest in union affairs. However, they have failed to address another important cause of labor force demoralization: that of powerlessness (Moore 1965, p. 44). Union centralization, leadership cooptation, government control over union activities and finance, loss of union voice in the determination of wages and working conditions, and loss of effective grievance machinery result in the disenfranchising of workers from participation in decisions affecting their welfare and worklives. Unions become arms of government rather than representatives of worker interests.

Popular-authoritarian corporatism is an attempt to enhance the commitment and loyalty of workers to unions, enterprises, and institutional norms through limited forms of participation in economic decision making. In order to understand such a corporatist pattern, it is useful to begin with O'Donnell's (1977) distinction between "statizing" corporatism, in which government penetrates outside groups and controls them without incorporating them into the ruling structures, and "privatizing" corporatism, in which nongovernmental groups are incorporated into the state and given specific, controlled roles within that structure. This conceptual distinction provides the basis for distinguishing between "bureaucratic" and "popular" forms of authoritarian corporatism.

The various types of state-labor relationships discussed thus far, based on whether the state controls unions and whether unions have gained a voice in policy and economic decision making, are shown in Figure 1.1. Collective bargaining (cell #1) involves little interpenetration between unions and state, while cell #2, bureaucratic-authoritarian corporatism, involves state controls over unions without their inclusion in decision making. Cell #3, populism, is a situation in which unions or other nongovernmental groups have penetrated government institutions without procedural constraint. This is a situation of uncontrolled politicization which typically results in political instability. Finally, cell #4, popular-authoritarian corporatism, involves at least limited penetration of elite decision making by groups which are subject to elite control and which thus do not threaten political instability or challenge established policies and institutions.

Bureaucratic and popular forms of authoritarian corporatism are similar in many respects, given their shared authoritarian emphasis on state control over the organization and activities of popular groups. They differ primarily in the relative emphasis given control on one hand and mobilization of controlled participation on the other. Such participation may involve limited union participation in national policy formulation or involvement in middle-level decision making relating to the implementation of industrial policy. It typically takes the form of information or petition rather than of autonomous bargaining and is responded to at the full discretion of policy makers who remain largely insulated from political pressures (Kaufman 1977).

Popular forms of authoritarian corporatism also occur at the organizational level as suggested by the instituting of human relations management, works councils, and grievance procedures. In some cases such limited forms of worker participation in enterprise-level decision making is in response to government pressure or encouragement. More often, it is an attempt to deal with the negative economic consequences of low morale among workers. Kannappan (1968) notes that while wages and benefits are readily controllable by elites, performance is not. This, he argues, means that strong wage controls often lead to recognition of a need for works councils, grievance processing, and other efforts to boost worker morale. In addition, as industrial technology grows more sophisticated and increases the need for extensive in-plant training of workers, employers begin to search for ways of securing a more stable workforce. One effective way to do this is through the elaboration of mechanisms through which workers can voice their grievances other than by quitting.

FIGURE 1.1

State Control of Unions

		Low	High
Labor penetration of government	Low	(1) collective bargaining	(2) bureaucratic- authoritarian corporatism
	High	(3) populism	(4) popular- authoritarian corporatism

An excellent example of an apparently stable and effective popular-authoritarian system is that of Mexico. Following President Cardenas' reorganization of nonelite groups in Mexican society into four state-controlled sectors, employers and unions have been brought into a stable corporate system of participation and representation in government decision making. Employers are required to join national-level confederations of commerce and industry and to deal with government bodies exclusively through these government-controlled chambers. Similarly, a single trade union federation, the CTM, represents labor interests through participation in the ruling national political party, the PRI, as well as in the Chamber of Deputies, where labor is granted a fixed number of seats. The

PRI functions to mobilize popular support through closely regulated elections, while the Chamber of Deputies permits labor interest representation in an executive dominated national government structure. Participation by both business and labor interests in the Mexican system is viewed as a privilege granted by government elites, and labor has, according to Kassalow (1969), become a reliable part of the ruling party.

If popular-authoritarian corporatist regimes attempt to create a viable associational base for institutional norms and policy, they must also ensure that such support does not politicize popular groups with respect to basic policy and elite structures. Patrimonialism, dependency on the state for group recognition and the right to represent group interests, and continuing authoritarian controls over union activities and leadership were noted earlier as effective means by which to control and channel participation. But a further, and more thoroughgoing, if rare, approach to control is through the creation of truly corporate structures, or vertical, functional interest associations among whom interrelations are mediated by a national center. In economic life such associations might take the form of industrial associations composed of both workers and employers, as initially suggested by Durkheim in his proposal that national integration be achieved through the formation of corporations in major economic sectors (1933, pp. 23-28). Such a proposal was in fact instituted in the European fascist experiments of the 1930s (Collier and Collier 1977). From the standpoint of industrial relations, such corporations would diffuse and reduce the conflict between labor and management, integrate labor into economic and political elite structures, and undercut horizontal, class-based opposition to elite policy. While third world countries have rarely extended corporatism this far, they have moved toward more limited forms. At the cultural level, of course, unitary, nationalist ideologies of economic development and social unity have asserted the identity of basic values and goals among all social groups and classes. And structurally, a number of corporatist experiments have been attempted. Peru, for instance, has legally mandated the creation of Industrial Communities consisting of all employees of large business firms. These communities are jointly governed by managers and workers and acquire collective ownership and managing control over the firms through a progressive distribution of profits in the form of shares both to the community and to its individual members. The 1970 legislation relating to the formation of such Industrial Communities makes clear its corporatist intent: "to strengthen the industrial undertaking by the unitary action of the workers in management, in the production process, in the property of the undertaking and in reinvestment, and by means of stimulating constructive forms of interrelation between capital and labor" (quoted in Pasara and Santistevan 1973). Increasingly, it is anticipated, industrial communities will provide a basis for participation in economic decision making at both enterprise and national levels, and the group-interest representation role of unions will be reduced.

To some extent, of course, the earlier mentioned forms of limited worker participation in decision making involve attempts to replace horizontal, class-based attachments with vertical commitments relating to works councils, human relations programs, joint participation by union and employer representatives on national advisory boards and commissions, and encouragement of enterprise-level bargaining within policy guidelines established by national union leaders.

Despite the failure of such earlier attempts to create effective popular-authoritarian corporatist systems as those of Velasco in Peru, Peron in Argentina, Vargas in Brazil, and Nkrumah in Ghana, as well as the frequent degeneration of such systems into uncontrolled populism, some writers have begun to argue that given the problems of labor force demoralization under bureaucratic-authoritarian regimes there will be renewed efforts to broaden the political base of such regimes through increased popular participation. Under the assumption that industrialization and modernization suggest a continuing tendency toward increased politicization (Chalmers 1977), Schoutz (1978) argues that "the ubiquitous nature of social and political mobilization suggests that popular authoritarianism [of the Peronist variety] may become increasingly common, providing the principal alternative to both bureaucratic-authoritarianism and social revolution." Similarly, Kassalow (1969) suggests that Mexico may present a viable model for state-union relations in other developing countries.

AUTHORITARIAN CORPORATISM AND WORLD MARKET ORIENTED INDUSTRIALIZATION

Case of KOREA

Much of the literature on the social and economic impact of foreign investment in third world countries deals largely with traditional investments in such areas as mining, petroleum, plantation agriculture, and related extractive, processing, transport and financing activities where foreign companies have found it necessary to introduce outside capital and technology to facilitate the effective exploitation of locally available natural resources. Much of this investment, though not all, has been relatively capital-intensive.

Apter (1976), O'Donnell (1977), and Collier and Collier (1977) have noted the close relationship between such dependent development and authoritarian corporatism. In part, the relationship may be explained by the fact that the imposition of authoritarian rule, often with military backing, provides a political climate conducive to foreign investment. Brazil's recent "economic miracle," for example, was based largely on the wave of foreign investment which followed the 1964 rightist military coup (Shankman 1979).

A second type of explanation for this relationship, and one which will be developed in this study, relates to the ways in which the socioeconomic consequences of dependent industrialization may be associated with an extension and consolidation of authoritarian corporatism. First, dependent development is often associated with an attenuation in the strength and independence of local business classes. This results from an undercutting of local enterprise by foreign firms (United Nations 1974, chapter 3; Turner 1973, chapter 3; International Labour Organization 1973, p. 48), a preempting by outside investors of high profit economic sectors, lack of backward economic linkages or of technology transfer in the context of "enclave" development (Furtado 1970, p. 251), and a growing external dependency of local entrepreneurs who increasingly assume commercial, subcontracting, and supplier roles vis-a-vis multinational firms (Frank 1972, p. 38). Such a weakening of the domestic bourgeoisie, it may be argued, reduces the likelihood of effective middle-class political opposition to authoritarian rule.

A second consequence of dependent development is a shift of the economic resource base of government from local to international firms and a resulting insulation of ruling elites from local interest groups (Frank 1972; Chase-Dunn 1975; Galtung 1971). Such growing independence of ruling elites vis-a-vis local groups increases the political autonomy of such elites in the national economy.

Capital-intensive foreign investment in third world countries is often associated with the emergence of a "labor aristocracy" consisting of those workers who are employed in the foreign sector and command relatively high wages (International Labour Organization 1973, chapter 3; Harris 1975). The employment and income dependency of this labor aristocracy on foreign firms as well as on the political framework which protects foreign investment reduces the likelihood of political opposition on the part of organized labor (Apter 1976, p. 27).

Finally, it is frequently noted that the economic benefits of dependent development accrue disproportionately to a few regions and population groups (Furtado 1970), thus generating growing economic inequality (Chase-Dunn 1975; Furtado 1970; Shankman 1979). Apter argues that the political instability engendered by such inequality and other forms of social disruption attendant upon dependent development may encourage increasing political authoritarianism in order to forestall political disorder. It should be noted, however, that the growing reliance of political elites on military coercion suggests a longer-term instability in such regimes.

Foreign investment in third world countries has more recently shifted to a greater emphasis on cost factors, especially those relating to labor (Solomon 1978, p. 12). Encouraged by technological changes permitting the breaking down of complex production processes into simple subroutines, as well as by growing labor costs and conflict in industrial countries, this new wave of "world market oriented" industrialization (Frobel et al. 1980, III), based on such labor-intensive industries as electronics, wearing apparel, plastics, and photographic equipment, has been associated with the rapid development of free-export-processing zones in a number of third world countries such as Mexico, Singapore, South Korea, and Taiwan. Such zones now employ large numbers of low-skilled workers in simple assembly operations in over half the developing countries (Frobel et al. 1980, III). Firms of this sort typically import materials and equipment from other countries and then reexport the semifinished or finished products for further processing or final sale elsewhere.

If capital-intensive foreign investment encourages generalized authoritarian political controls, labor-intensive investment focuses the need for such control in the industrial relations arena. In order to maintain competitive labor costs, and thus to attract foreign investment, governments typically impose strict wage controls and restrict the freedom of unions to bargain and to engage in collective action (Frobel et al. 1980, III; International Labour Organization 1973, p. 85). In addition, the more specifically corporatist aspects of such control center on efforts to transform trade unions into instruments of political discipline and socialization. Illustrative of the stress placed on corporatist labor controls in order to attract foreign manufacturing investment is Taiwan's recent and dramatic industrialization experience. Taiwan's success in attracting foreign capital, which accounted for two-thirds of total manufacturing investment during the period 1969-76 (Bellows 1976), was strongly encouraged by tight government controls over wages and industrial conflict (Thompson 1976), a general displacement of collective bargaining by government arbitration, and close surveillance of organized labor, particularly in Taiwan's free-export-processing zones.

In addition, and to a far greater degree than in the case of the traditional pattern of dependent development, the socioeconomic consequences of world market oriented industrialization tend to enhance the long-run stability of authoritarian corporatism. As in the former case, local enterprise often may either be displaced or tied into bonds of economic dependency vis-a-vis foreign firms. Similarly, the economic resource base of ruling elites shifts from local to foreign business. But because of the greater employment impact of world market oriented industry, the social impact of such investment on labor may be quite different. By generating employment for large numbers of low-skilled workers, industrialization is less likely either to create a labor aristocracy or to substantially increase economic inequality (Adelman and Robinson 1978, pp. 192-93). World market oriented industrialization may also spawn an industrial labor force characterized by social atomism and low solidarity, and thus largely unable to organize against economic and political elites. This results from such characteristics of industrial employment as low job security (International Labour Organization 1973), high rates of job mobility (Shankman 1979), and disproportionate growth in the "secondary" employment sector. Finally, the tendency for foreign investment to concentrate in a few key export industries tends to support the consolidation of the labor movement into a highly centralized trade union structure, thus facilitating an intensification of corporatist control. In these various ways, it may be argued, world market oriented industrialization may enhance the legitimacy and long-run stability of authoritarian corporatism.

While growth in Taiwan's dynamic agricultural sector has tended to mask the direct sociopolitical consequences of world market oriented industrialization, the South Korean case brings these out more clearly. Korea's industrial progress has been spectacular by world and historical standards. In 12 years (1960-72) manufacturing as a percentage of total GNP increased from 11 percent to 26 percent while agriculture declined from 41 percent to 25 percent. And during this same period, the percentage of employment in manufacturing increased from 8.7 percent to 14.1 percent of the total. More important, mining and manufacturing accounted for 35.3 percent of the growth in employment between 1963 and 1972, versus only 4.2 percent for agriculture (Hasan 1976). The average real GNP growth rate for the period 1959-62 was 3.6 percent per annum, while that for 1963-74 was 10 percent. Per capita annual income doubled to $470 (U.S.) during that period, thereafter growing to $700 in 1976. And, finally, rapid economic growth was reflected in a decline in unemployment from 8.5 percent in 1963 to 4.1 percent in 1974 (Hasan 1976).

Manufacturing, which has provided the basis for Korea's spectacular economic growth, has been mainly export oriented, as seen in the increase of exports as a percentage of GNP from 2.4 percent in 1962 to 30.8 percent in 1976 (Kim 1978). And lacking a viable agricultural or natural resource base for domestic capital generation, Korean industry has had to rely extensively on foreign capital. It has been estimated that foreign capital financed approximately 45 percent of total investment for the two five-year plans of 1962-67 and 1967-71 (Tae 1972). During the early 1960s, capital inflows consisted predominantly of official grants and aid, while during the second half of the decade emphasis shifted to commercial and official concessionary loans.

Much Korean industrial enterprise has, since the early 1950s, been in the hands of large financial and business empires comparable, in some ways, to the Japanese zaibatsu. These empires, with substantial control over major economic sectors, have in turn depended heavily on government support. Much of this dependence stems from a continuing need for loans through government-controlled commercial banks which act as intermediaries between foreign capital and local businessmen. Conversely, through contracts and control over the distribution of foreign aid and capital loans, government has nurtured growth in a few major companies through which it has implemented its industrial development programs. Very recently, this previously informal arrangement has been formalized in the statutory specification of criteria in terms of which businesses can qualify as General Trading Companies eligible for low-interest industrial loans. Qualification criteria include trade penetration of a specified number of countries in different regions of the world and a minimum yearly export volume, neither of which are within reach of any but the largest companies. And it is these companies which have greatest initial access to foreign and commercial financing to meet the new qualifications in the first place.

In part because of an increasing debt-service burden, the government has more recently shifted to greater stress on direct foreign investment. This new emphasis began with the Foreign Capital Inducement Law of 1966 which created a number of tax and other incentives for foreign investment. In 1970, the government created an Economic Planning Board to coordinate government activities relating to foreign investment and established free-export-production zones at Masan and Iri for foreign and foreign majority owned, export oriented firms. By 1974, 27 such industrial estates were operational. Finally, in 1972, increasing emphasis on direct foreign investment was reflected in a new Foreign Capital Inducement Law under which the government guaranteed repayment on foreign loans, eliminated remaining restrictions on the remittance of profits by foreign firms, guaranteed protection of property, and increased tax incentives for foreign investors (Tae 1972). As a result of these and other steps, foreign direct investment increased from $29.3 million (U.S.) in 1968 to $263.7 million in 1973. And given the strategic importance of industrial exports for Korean economic growth, it is significant that in 1973 foreign and joint-venture firms accounted for 69 percent of total exports, versus only 15 percent in 1971 (Cohen 1975), while exports, in turn, comprised over 80 percent of total manufacturing output.

More than 70 percent of the new direct foreign investment has been in manufacturing, and much of this has been in such labor-intensive industries as electronics, textiles, wearing apparel, machinery, and metal industries (Suh 1976). It is thus not surprising that Korea's rapid industrialization has been strongly encouraged by tight controls on organized labor. Collective bargaining is seen as a threat to foreign as well as local investment (Kim 1975) and has largely been supplanted by government "compulsory mediation" (McDiarmid 1977). Under emergency rule, strikes are effectively reduced (Far Eastern Economic Review 11/1/74) and are actually illegal among public employees and in free-export-processing zones (Frobel et al. 1977). Direct government control of unions is illustrated by the successful 1974 imposition, through election manipulation, of a government-backed candidate for chairman of the Federation of Korean Trade Unions, the only officially recognized union federation. Following the election, the Korean Central Intelligence Agency simply muffled the protests of several union presidents.

But if labor controls have stimulated industrial investment, the resulting pattern of world market oriented industrialization has in turn helped to stabilize and solidify Korea's bureaucratic-authoritarian corporatism. First, government access to investment and aid resources from politically neutral outside sources reduces political vulnerability to local political pressures. Second, export oriented firms, both foreign and domestic, are integrated less into the domestic economy than into an international economic division of labor. A high percentage of both capital goods and raw materials are imported, while most output is shipped abroad. Korea's modern industrial sector increasingly comprises a dynamic economic enclave within a larger relatively stagnant economy. The relative stagnation in domestically and privately capitalized indigenous enterprise has forestalled the emergence of an independent business class which might have pressed for political liberalization.

Third, the rapid growth of new industrial estates has minimized the potential of established industrial communities to provide a source of labor organization and leadership independent of government control. Related to this is an atomization of the labor force in modern industry, as suggested by very high resignation rates, low rates of union organization (McDiarmid 1977), and low morale and apathy (Frobel et al. 1980, III) Officially sanctioned labor unions, conversely, have been readily centralized in the context of large-scale enterprise and export concentration in a few major industries.

In these ways, sociopolitical consequences of world market oriented industrialization, along with the rapid economic growth it has made possible, have reduced the potential for effective, organized opposition to political authoritarianism in Korea.

SINGAPORE AS A CASE STUDY IN WORLD
MARKET ORIENTED INDUSTRIALIZATION

In the following chapters we shall further explore the nature of the relationship between world market oriented industrialization and authoritarian corporatism through a case study of Singapore, a country which has recently gone through a period of very rapid industrialization, based heavily on foreign investment in labor-intensive industry. During this period of development, the ruling People's Action Party (PAP), led by Lee Kuan Yew, has pursued a highly successful corporatist strategy in its dealings with labor, so that today most unions in Singapore are affiliated with the National Trades Union Congress (NTUC), the only officially recognized union federation. The NTUC enjoys a very close relationship with the ruling party and has increasingly been able to participate in government decision making. In this and other respects, Singapore appears to be moving toward a popular-authoritarian mode of corporatism.

Singapore is in many respects a unique society in that it is primarily a small city-state with little rural hinterland. But far from detracting from the more general relevance of this case study to other industrializing societies, Singapore's very uniqueness is its advantage. Singapore's experience permits an examination of the relationship between a particular mode of industrialization and an evolving industrial relations system in isolation of confounding effects of urbanization, rural-urban resource transfers, opposition from rural elites, and other factors that normally accompany economic change in more complex and diversified societies. In this sense, Singapore provides a relatively easy case for the initial systematic study of this relationship and thus is a useful starting point for suggesting general principles which can subsequently be further explored through more comparative research.

2
PREINDUSTRIAL SINGAPORE:
THE COMMUNAL ECONOMY

This chapter provides a general social and economic background for the subsequent examination of Singapore's industrialization experience. During the colonial period, Singapore's dynamic entrepot economy was based strongly on emergent associational bonds of kinship, geographical origin, dialect, religion, and other primordial affiliations. Especially among the majority Chinese population, these associational bonds, initially focusing on kinship and village and later, during the early 1900s, on broader dialect and ethnic identities, provided the basis for the trust and reliability which was necessary for social and economic integration in a predominantly immigrant colonial society. It was largely on the basis of these associational loyalties that employment relations and labor unions were initially formed.

HISTORICAL BACKGROUND

The Republic of Singapore comprises a single large island and a number of small islets with a total land area of only 225 square miles at the southern tip of the Malayan peninsula. Singapore's modern history began with its selection by Stamford Raffles in 1819 as a future British maritime base. In 1824, under the Treaty of London, Singapore was ceded to the East India Company, and beginning in 1826 it became a Straits Settlement ruled, along with Penang and Malacca, from India. It was only in 1867 that Singapore became a British crown colony, ruled directly from London until the World War II Japanese occupation.

Under colonial rule, Singapore grew to be a major commercial, financial, and entrepot center for the region. This was the result in part of British policy under which trade duties were kept low and port facilities developed. But more important was Singapore's natural harbor and strategic location at the crossroads of Southeast Asian maritime trade. The trade potential of Singapore had been recognized at the outset by Raffles who, in 1819, wrote:

> The island of Sincapore [sic], independently of the straits and harbour of Johore, which it both forms and commands, has, on its southern shores, and by means of the several smaller islands which lie off it, excellent anchorage and smaller harbours. . . . Its position in the straits of Singapore is far more commanding than even Rhio, for our China trade passing down the Straits of Malacca, and every native vessel that sails through the Straits of Rhio must pass in sight of it (quoted in Ooi Jin-Bee 1969, p. 2).

A third factor underlying Singapore's development was the tremendous growth of trade and communication between Asia and Europe following the arrival of steam powered boats in 1845, the Australian gold rush of the early 1850s, and the opening of the Suez Canal in 1869 (Lee Soo Ann 1973).

Finally, and perhaps of greatest importance, was the regional development, during the early 1900s, of the tin and rubber industries of Malaya and Sumatra. These and such other commodities as petroleum, timber, and plantation crops encouraged Singapore's emerging role as a center for the processing and transshipment of regional products, as well for related banking, shipping, insurance, and storage services (Lee Soo Ann 1973). And Singapore's economic linkage particularly to Malaya's commodity production activities ensured its close integration with the larger peninsular economy. As late as the early 1960s, 57.4 percent of Singapore's total Gross Domestic Product was accounted for by trade, restaurants and hotels, transport, storage, communication, and finance (Singapore International Chamber of Commerce 1976).

Along with Singapore's development into a major regional entrepot center came rapid immigration of persons, first from various districts of China and later from India and Malaya, to seize new economic opportunities associated with growing needs for unskilled and skilled labor, traders and clerks, and a variety of other service workers in the expanding urban center. On the basis of such immigration, the population increased from almost nil at the time of Raffles' landing, to roughly 558,000 in 1931. An outstanding characteristic of this growing population has been its ethnic and cultural heterogeneity. Census figures show that by the 1930s Chinese constituted roughly 75 percent of the total population, while Malays constituted 13 percent and Indians 8 to 9 percent, figures that have not changed substantially up to more recent times (Chang 1976). But the true heterogeneity of the population becomes more readily apparent from detailed breakdowns of these three major groups into their ethnically distinct subcommunities. The 1970 census shows the Chinese to include 42.2 percent Hokkien, 22.4 percent Teochew, 17 percent Cantonese, 7 percent each of Hainanese and Hakka, and a number of other dialect and regional groups (Chang 1976). Similarly, the Malays include peninsular Malays, Javanese, and Boyanese, while Indians consist of Tamils, Malayalees, Punjabis, and several other smaller groups. In most cases, dialect and subgroups even within a single larger ethnic population of Chinese, Malays, or Indians, are separated from one another by language and other cultural barriers. Thus, in speaking particularly of the colonial population of Singapore, one must refer to a large aggregation of distinctive immigrant communities within the larger political entity.

THE ECONOMIC INTEGRATION OF IMMIGRANTS INTO SINGAPORE SOCIETY

During the 1800s, most of Singapore's predominantly immigrant workers either were single males or were married men who had left families at home in order to come to Singapore to earn their fortunes and then return home or send for wives and children. In most cases the immigrants were quite poor and lacked even passage money. This situation led to reliance by the colonial government and employers on the use of various systems of indenture and contractual bonding whereby passage fare would be prepaid, in return for which the immigrant would agree to work off his debt to his sponsor (Blythe 1947). Under one particularly abusive form of such labor recruitment, which came to be known as the "pig trade," labor recruiters would ship workers to Singapore and then keep them locked up or under close supervision until they could be "sold" to a local employer who would in turn be entitled to bonded service for some agreed upon period. Such a system continued through informal agreements even after 1910, when it was declared illegal by the colonial government (Bingham 1947). While this system of bonding and indenture was the single most important method of labor recruitment for the agricultural, rubber, and mining activities on the Malayan peninsula, it was also used by many employers in the City of Singapore itself in the recruitment of menial labor used on the docks and in private firms and warehouses. Particularly important in such early labor recruitment were Chinese secret societies. These societies both handled the actual recruitment and transport of laborers and later prevented workers from fleeing their recruiters or new employers (Mak 1978).

A striking characteristic of emerging economic patterns in Singapore was the tendency toward occupational specialization on the part of the various immigrant groups. A 1947 report from the Singapore Labour Department (Bingham 1947) listed the following types of work pursued by Chinese from various parts of south China:

Shanghai and Chekiang Province	carpenters, dry cleaners, dressmakers
Foochow and North Fukien Province	barbers, rickshaw pullers, trishaw pedallers, lorry drivers
Amoy and South Fukien Province	unskilled laborers, boatmen, fishermen, sawmillers
Swatow	vegetable gardeners
Kwangtung Province:	
(a) Hakkas	shoemakers, rattan furniture workers, quarry workers
(b) Cantonese	carpenters, mechanics, skilled workers
Hainan Island	rubber millers, bakers, sawmillers, domestic servants

This same report discussed the tendency for Sikhs and other North Indians to be watchmen and bus or lorry drivers, for Tamils to be light laborers in Public Works and the Municipality, and for Malays to work in menial positions in government. Even as late as 1964, the tendency for trade specialization among dialect groups within the Chinese population was still evident. Table 2.1 shows the distribution of 423 Chinese firms listed in the Chinese Chamber of Commerce Directory of 1964 for which information could be obtained on both major line of business and dialect group.* Because

---

*These data should be taken as suggestive only, since (1) information on the dialect affiliation of many firms was missing, (2) some firms hold chamber membership through trade associations rather than individually, and (3) numbers of firms in a given category are in part an artifact of varied and complex legal divisions of ownership in family firms.

Hokkiens are the numerically dominant Chinese dialect group in Singapore, Hokkien firms naturally dominate many of the lines of business in this table. Thus, it is appropriate to note those areas in which Hokkien and other firms are overrepresented relative to their percentage distribution in the total sample of firms (bottom row of the table). It may be seen that Hokkien firms are strongly overrepresented in shipping, rubber, rice and other foodstuffs, spices and tobacco, and artcrafts, and virtually monopolize the rubber and automobile/bicycle/tire trades. Similarly, Cantonese are overrepresented among clockmakers, jewellers, and goldsmiths, as well as in medical supplies, lumber, and engineering. Shanghai firms are overrepresented in cinemas, amusement facilities, and leather products, in each of which they hold a dominant position. Teochews are overrepresented in finance, palm oil products, and textiles; Hainanese in remittance shops and furniture; and Hakkas in clocks and jewelry, textiles, and medical supplies.

The experience of the Hengua dialect group,* from Fukien Province, illustrates the process of occupational specialization among even relatively more recent immigrants. Persons from this group began arriving after 1913 and at first found employment mainly as rickshaw and trishaw operators. As their economic position improved, they moved initially into retailing of bicycle parts and then, in the 1920s, into retailing of automotive parts and tires. Later, they established a strong position in the operation of city bus companies as well as in motor repairing and the tire trade. Once Henguas had obtained a strong position in tire, transportation, and related trades, recruitment into these trades tended increasingly to be from among other Henguas. After 1948 many new Hengua immigrants arrived in Singapore from China and were recruited as shopkeepers and apprentices within established Hengua trades (The Singapore Straits Times 1/25/77).

The tendency toward occupational specialization can be explained by a number of factors. First, the labor recruitment practices described earlier were largely confined to narrow groups of shared kinship or place of origin. This, along with the tendency for new immigrants who came as individuals to seek employment in the businesses of earlier immigrants from their own village or district, led naturally to increasing occupational specialization among the various groups. Other factors include preimmigration experience and skills, language and dialect barriers, available opportunities at the time of arrival of particular groups, and the exigencies of

---

*Henguas are included in the Hokkien category in the Chamber membership listing.

TABLE 2.1

Firms Listed in 1964 Chinese Chamber of Commerce Directory
by Dialect Group and Line of Business

Line of Business	Total Number of Firms in Each Line	Hokkien Firms		Cantonese Firms	
		No.	% of Firms in Line	No.	% of Firms in Line
Shipping	19	18	95	1	5
Shipping agents	40	35	86	0	—
Rubber	36	34	84	0	—
Plantations, mines, property	13	9	69	1	8
Rice and foodstuffs	41	32	78	1	2
Beverages	12	9	75	0	—
Finance	13	5	38	2	15
Auto, bikes, tires	15	15	100	0	—
Clocks, jewelry, gold	12	2	17	7	58
Clothing, textiles	31	9	29	7	23
Medical supplies	26	2	8	13	50
Paper products	17	8	47	1	6
Building, contracting	18	9	50	1	6
Hardware supplies	44	29	66	5	11
Lumber	5	2	40	2	40
Engineering works	8	2	25	3	38
Tobacco, spices, coffee	25	19	76	4	16
Sauces	6	4	67	2	33
Food preparation and restaurants	10	7	70	0	—
Furniture	8	3	38	1	13
Books, printing	12	2	17	3	25
Cinema and amusement	19	1	5	0	—
Leather products	4	1	25	0	—
Artcrafts, antiques	4	3	75	0	—
Optical goods	3	0	—	0	—
Travel agents	4	1	25	0	—
Palm based soap, oils	12	8	67	0	—
Remittance shops	13	2	15	3	23
Total number of firms	423*	251	59	53	13

*The sum of the firms in the various lines of business is greater than the total number of firms because one firm may engage in more than one type of business.

Source: Chinese Chamber of Commerce, Singapore.

Shanghai Firms		Teochew Firms		Hainanese Firms		Hakka Firms	
No.	% of Firms in Line	No.	% of Firms in Line	No.	% of Firms in Line	No.	% of Firms in Line
0	—	0	—	0	—	0	—
1	3	3	8	1	3	0	—
0	—	1	3	1	3	0	—
1	8	0	—	1	8	1	8
0	—	7	17	0	—	1	2
1	8	0	—	2	17	0	—
1	8	5	38	0	—	0	—
0	—	0	—	0	—	0	—
0	—	1	8	0	—	2	17
1	3	9	29	0	—	5	16
0	—	4	15	3	12	4	15
4	24	3	18	0	—	1	6
7	39	0	—	1	6	0	—
7	16	1	2	1	2	1	2
1	20	0	—	0	—	0	—
3	38	0	—	0	—	0	—
0	—	1	4	1	4	0	—
0	—	0	—	0	—	0	—
2	20	0	—	1	10	0	—
2	25	0	—	2	25	0	—
6	50	0	—	1	8	0	—
18	95	0	—	0	—	0	—
3	75	0	—	0	—	0	—
1	25	0	—	0	—	0	—
0	—	0	—	0	—	3	100
0	—	0	—	1	25	2	50
0	—	4	33	0	—	0	—
0	—	1	8	6	46	1	8
49	12	38	9	15	4	17	4

colonial recruitment at particular places and times for specific
labor requirements.

But of equal importance was the tendency for different resi-
dent groups to seek exclusive control over their trades through both
legal and illegal organization (Purcell 1951; Awbery and Dalley 1948).
Within the Chinese community, most trades within the major dialect
groups came to be tightly organized through dialect-specific guilds
and trade associations (Suyama 1962). The two primary functions of
such associations were to organize and regulate commerce and to
reduce competition or maintain group monopolization of given trades.

The rubber trade provides an excellent example of the importance of such associations in commercial life. As noted earlier,
the Hokkiens have traditionally dominated many phases of the rubber
trade. This they have accomplished through the development of a
network of close personal relationships among Hokkiens involved in
all stages of the rubber trade: from plantation and upland traders
through truckers and buyers, to warehouse owners, financiers,
processors, and shippers. This integrated trade network was organized only in part on the basis of ramifying kinship ties. More
important by far were the many associations and trade guilds developed by Hokkiens and others to regulate various aspects and stages
of the trade such as pricing, competition, standards, contracts,
credit, shipping, and even entry into the trade itself. Most of these
associations operated under the aegis of the Singapore Chamber of
Commerce Rubber Association (Wilson 1958). Misrepresentation,
fraud, or violation of association rules would result in exclusion
from the rubber trade. Such exclusion would in turn result not only
in loss of face but in most cases financial ruin as well, since one's
credit standing, an important basis for commercial dealings in a
capital-poor economy, would be destroyed. Since many of the trade
associations relating to particular aspects of the rubber trade were
effectively controlled by Hokkiens, later immigrant groups, such as
the Hainanese, found it difficult to break into the trade and had to
move into other, less lucrative, fields (Lim 1958).

It should also be mentioned that secret societies, in addition
to their earlier mentioned role in labor recruitment and control,
also served well into the twentieth century to help establish and de-
fend trade and artisan monopolies on behalf of the memberships of
the larger associations with which they were affiliated.

THE EMERGENCE OF ECONOMIC COMMUNITIES

As employers of shared dialect and in related trades tended
to locate in particular areas of the city, immigrants sought housing

accommodation near their new places of employment.* By consequence, existing tendencies toward geographical segregation were
greatly strengthened, and distinct dialect neighborhoods emerged,
particularly in Singapore's old Chinatown area. This process was
further encouraged by British efforts to create largely self-contained
ethnic quarters in order to minimize intergroup conflict (Purcell
1975). Kaye (1960) studied one such neighborhood, along Upper
Nanking Street, during the 1950s. Residents of this predominantly
Cantonese district were mainly employed in construction, hawking,
medicines, textiles, engineering, garment making, paper manufacture, motor servicing, and other skilled artisan occupations in
which Cantonese have traditionally been strongly represented. Most
of these residents lived quite close to their place of employment and
in many cases were given room and board by their employers or received lodging and community assistance within the trade district
where they worked. The more general pattern of commercially
based spatial segregation among Chinese dialect groups was described by Neville:

> Among the Chinese, several of the larger communities
> have long retained a strong identity with certain locali-
> ties particularly within the central city area. The
> Hokkien community was located mainly in the older
> parts of Chinatown in a zone close to the Singapore
> River and the coast, and near the business areas; the
> location reflects the dominance of the Hokkien immi-
> grants in early Singapore and amongst Chinese mer-
> chants. The Teochew community was concentrated
> mainly on the south bank of the Singapore River in a
> very compact area. Occupational specialization was
> again a factor as many Teochews were employed in the
> transfer of goods between riverside warehouses and
> tongkangs or lighters crowding the river. Teochews
> have also specialized in some sectors of the inter-
> island boat trade, dealing especially with west Borneo
> and south Thailand where there are substantial Teochew
> trading communities. The Cantonese have been arti-
> sans of all types, and have no great need of a location
> suitable for commercial activities; they were concen-

---

*The 1964 membership rolls of the Chinese Chamber of Com-
merce show distinct ethnic and trade concentrations along particular
streets in Singapore's now renovated central commercial district.

trated in a large area away from the river on the
southward side (Ooi and Chiang 1969, p. 59).

On the basis of such demographic and economic processes
emerged Singapore's ethnically homogeneous economic neighborhoods.

COMMUNAL ECONOMY AND SOCIAL ORDER

In Singapore's capital-poor commercial society of immigrants,
economic cooperation was the basis for survival. The overriding
importance of access to employment and economic opportunity ensured the central significance of economic associations in immigrant
settlement areas (Mak 1978). These associations, in turn, became
the basis for the provision of a wide range of community services
that the colonial government failed to provide. That such associations were intimately bound up with the evolution and success of the
communal economy ensured that communalism would extend beyond
economic life to social, political, and cultural affairs as well.

As noted earlier, corresponding to the territorial economic
community was a network of dependency relations: of those lacking
education, wealth, or jobs on those who might provide these, either
directly, or more often indirectly, through associations, in exchange
for status, recognition, power, or services. Of foremost importance, perhaps, were those economic associations that, in the first
instance, were established to ensure economic order. Guilds, trade
associations, chambers of commerce, and other such organizations
were financed and managed by established businessmen. Through
such associations, these businessmen established contacts, pro-
tected their economic interests, established and maintained economic relationships and reputations (and thus their continuing access to credit), and in other ways ensured the smooth functioning of
local business (Carstens 1975).

The dynamic communal economy provided the material foundation for the sociocultural integration of dialect and ethnic communities. During the early 1900s, dialect associations began to rival in
importance the clan, trade, and other narrower and often economically oriented associations which had developed earlier. Between
1910 and 1926, the Singapore Foochow Association (North Fukien),
the Chang Chow General Association (South Fukien), the Teochew
Association, and the Nanyang Khek Community Guild were established by persons of common regional or provincial origins in China
(Yong 1968). These associations, in turn, provided services and institutional support to community members. While clan and guild

organizations provided family assistance, observed festive holidays, provided burial services, maintained cemeteries, and gave educational support to deserving children of members, the dialect associations provided free public medical care through hospitals and clinics, and established libraries, clubs, recreational facilities, and, most important, schools and colleges. Ngee Ann College, a two-year vocational college, and Nanyang University, the only private four-year university in Singapore, were built by Teochew and Hokkien community associations respectively. And such associations, along with the community facilities they supported, received financial and other assistance from successful merchants and tradesmen who thus converted economic resources into community status and prestige, as exemplified in the numerous pictures of financial sponsors adorning the walls of local hospitals and other service institutions in Chinese areas. In these ways, growing economic wealth was channeled into community institutions that in turn bound community members more and more tightly together.

The most important city-wide Chinese association was the Singapore Chinese Chamber of Commerce. The Chamber was established by Chinese merchants in 1906 to safeguard Chinese commercial interests, mediate disputes within the Chinese community, and represent the community before the colonial government. The Chamber is essentially a federation of business groups from the various dialect communities. Its board of directors consists of members from each such community proportionate to its population. Chamber membership is held not only by individual persons and businesses but by trade associations as well, and the Chamber is involved in education, social welfare, and fund raising for a variety of public and charitable needs.

An excellent example of the commercial basis of a non–Chinese ethnic community is provided by Ibrahim's study (1977) of the Dawoodi Bohra Muslims. The early immigrants from this group specialized in the spice and timber trades and established close commercial and social bonds among themselves. In addition, they established a community organization, the Dawat, to control local expenditures for welfare, religious activities, industrial development schemes, and transfers of property. Through this and other community organizations, wealth is channeled into public institutions and facilities, while contacts outside the community, especially with government, are handled largely through the Singapore Dawoodi Bohra Association. The commercial prosperity of this community ensures that young males can readily find employment within local firms, so that communal loyalty is strengthened by the commercial opportunities, contacts, and capital available exclusively to community members.

Finally, it must be noted that while most of Singapore's dialect and ethnic communities developed largely on the basis of economic needs and mutual assistance, some communities evolved on a different basis. This is particularly true of the Malay community, which is integrated less by networks of economic dependency than by Muslim religious beliefs. From early colonial days the British treated the Malays as a special group in Malaya and Singapore, since they were considered the "native" inhabitants. The British in a sense became the guardians of Malay traditional life through support for Malay leadership, special consideration for Malays in government employment, recognition of Malay adat (customary law) and religious institutions, provision of Malay housing settlements, and support for Malay vernacular education. These special advantages have even encouraged other groups, such as the Batak, to assimilate into the Malay community (Chew 1978).

The cohesiveness of Singapore's Malay community thus derives less from economic interdependency than from government policy and religious solidarity. Malay workers, unlike their Chinese counterparts, are disproportionately represented among lower level workers in police, fire, postal, and other public services (Hanna 1966), while community organizations center less on economic activities than on cultural, religious, welfare, sports, literary, and educational interests and problems. It is these broadly cultural organizations that unite and define the Malay community of Singapore.

EMPLOYMENT RELATIONS IN SINGAPORE'S COMMUNAL ECONOMY

With the development of an increasingly adequate local labor supply and the emergence of integrated dialect communities, the recruitment and control of labor shifted from reliance on largely coercive control of immigrant indentured labor to greater emphasis on occupational guilds, labor subcontracting systems, and personal recommendation systems.

Guilds had been established in Singapore as far back as the mid-1800s and consisted of members generally of single dialect or locality groups engaged in particular trades or crafts. Such guilds, consisting of both employers and workers, acted to regulate prices, arbitrate disputes, reduce competition, maintain standards, preserve craft lore and skills, fix numbers of apprentices, and provide sickness and death benefits to members (Gamba 1962). Guilds may still be found among goldsmiths, carpenters, and dry goods merchants, though they increasingly confine themselves to social and mutual benefit activities (Gamba 1962). For larger undertakings requiring the hiring and supervision of many workers, particularly in boat building and construction, casual labor was recruited through "kepala," or skilled workers, who themselves recruited and supervised other workers engaged in a particular trade (for example, concrete work, bricklaying, and so forth). Each kepala would hire, train, and supervise his workers, and move his workgroup from worksite to worksite, depending on his luck in procuring jobs from developers and building contractors. Recruitment by such kepala, who often effectively dominated specific labor categories, led naturally to monopolization of recruitment and apprenticeship opportunities in many building trades by particular dialect groups (Republic of Singapore 1962). It also ensured tight authority and discipline among workers who were dependent on their kepala for obtaining work. The importance of such dependency is brought out in Kay's study (1973) of Singapore stevedores. Such workers were recruited, paid, and directed on the job by mandores, each of whom organized a "gang" of stevedores whose labor was hired out to contractors. In many cases, both mandores and stevedores were members of the same kongsi-houses, meeting places to facilitate labor recruitment and contacts. Where such common membership existed, workgangs developed closer bonds of loyalty to their mandores, exhibited lower rates of turnover, were more often unionized, and were more productive on the job than were gangs without such attachments.

THE SMALL CHINESE FIRM

Until the late 1960s, the majority of Singapore's business firms were small retail establishments employing fewer than five persons (Gamer 1972, chapter 6). A large proportion of employees worked in economically marginal cottage industries set up in semipermanent, low rental buildings. These firms minimized operating costs through provision of living space on the grounds in lieu of more adequate wages; use of free family labor; noncompliance with safety, copyright and labeling laws; use of oil lamps rather than electricity; and reliance on social obligations of friendship and kinship to obtain a variety of facilities and services which would otherwise have had to be purchased or hired (Gamer 1972).

In Singapore's immigrant and largely laissez faire economy, even well established businessmen exercised extreme caution in their management and employment practices. Ownership was confined to one or a few families, with great reluctance to pull in outside capital or additional partners. Decisions were centralized among top-level managers, with very little downward delegation of authority (Mok 1973; Lum 1974; Lau 1974), which was a consequence of stress on tight family control over business activities, lack of trust of outsiders, and a resulting emphasis on organizational security and restriction of access to information (Deyo 1978). Even today such caution manifests itself in a number of ways in employment relations within these firms. First, recruitment practices reflect a greater concern for trustworthiness and potential loyalty than for competence or formal training (Yong 1973). For management positions relatives or close friends are preferred, a practice which has the additional advantage of substantially reducing employee salary expenditures (Low 1973). For recruitment to nonmanagerial positions, an earlier reliance on guilds and kongsis gave way to the use of personal recommendations by close friends or by employees, especially those at supervisory levels. Such recommendations ensured that employee discipline and loyalty would be anchored in obligation either to immediate superiors or to a third party (Heyzer 1974). Advancement to supervisory positions was based less on formal education than on seniority and experience in the firm itself, and personal bonds of dependency between employers and workers was ensured through readily available personal loans to keep employees in debt (Cheng 1968), a frequent bypassing of supervisors by managers in their dealings with workers (Deyo 1978), highly discretionary wage increases and bonuses, and frequent off-the-job social contacts between employers and workers at funerals, weddings, New Year's celebrations, and other festive occasions.

THE BEGINNINGS OF ORGANIZED LABOR

Singapore's modern trade unions are largely a post-World War II phenomenon. Their origins lie in the guilds, clubs, and societies that, in sympathetic response to the growing labor movement in China during 1924-27, began to form exclusively among employees (Awbery and Dalley 1948). As late as 1939 government labor registers show only 92 employee guilds or unions, against 144 guilds containing both employees and employers. Employee unions appeared first among Chinese skilled mechanics (for example, The Chinese Engineering Mechanics Association) and clerical workers (for example, the Clerical Union). Most such unions were house unions and were generally dominated by employers.

The labor movement received strong impetus during World War II, when the local resistance movement stimulated underground labor mobilization against Japanese occupational forces. In part stemming from this wartime mobilization, leftist unions subsequently opposed the reestablishment of British colonial rule after the war. In response to increasingly alarming union militance culminating in antigovernment demonstrations during 1946, the British responded with detention of union leaders, union deregistration, and restriction of the use of union funds for political activities. Controls over organized labor were further increased following the 1948 declaration of national emergency in connection with growing Communist insurgency on the peninsula. At this point most opposition leaders were forced underground, and strike activity declined sharply. The British, meanwhile, began to organize a progovernment union federation, the Singapore Trades Union Congress (STUC), which was formally registered in 1951 and headed by an appointed English-speaking Secretary-General. Such labor controls closely anticipated the labor policy of Singapore's postindependence government during its period of political consolidation during the early 1960s.

A second period of labor politicization occurred in the mid and late 1950s during the transition to internal self-rule. This was a period of intense political competition and lobbying as various groups and elites sought to control Singapore's future political course. In part, the new wave of labor activism was a consequence of the successful efforts of the People's Action Party (PAP) to mobilize support among leftist, Chinese-educated, and labor groups in their efforts to win the 1959 election and thus to form Singapore's first locally autonomous government.

LEFTIST DEMOBILIZATION AND POLITICAL CONSOLIDATION

The PAP gained power with the support of a loose coalition of anglicized nationalist moderates and Chinese oriented leftists. During the postelection period, growing friction between these two wings of the ruling party finally led to a formal split, with the leftists breaking away to form their own party, the Barisan Socialis, or Socialist Party. Given the close links between the PAP and labor groups that had been mobilized during the election campaign, it was inevitable that the party split would spill over into industrial conflict. In fact, the PAP-Barisan split was reflected in the bifurcation of the STUC into a PAP-aligned National Trades Union Congress (NTUC) and a Barisan-aligned Singapore Association of Trade Unions (SATU). The PAP, like its British predecessors during the late 1940s, then set out to demobilize the SATU and its affiliated leftist trade unions through political detention of leaders, union deregistration, and harassment and surveillance of leftist labor organizers, culminating in 1963 in two major police swoops that all but eliminated remaining pockets of resistance (Chan 1976). This crackdown led to a reduction of work stoppages by roughly 90 percent between 1963 and 1964 and eliminated open political opposition among labor.

The demobilization of organized labor was but part of a broader process of depoliticization of leftist groups throughout Singapore. According to official Internal Security Department records, virtually all the front organizations for the Malayan Communist Party operative in Singapore during 1954-66 were to be found among Chinese educational and cultural associations and trade unions (Lee Ting Hui 1976). Thus, it was clear from the outset that Chinese communalism and Chinese nationalism were the organizational and cultural sources of political opposition to rule by a highly anglicized PAP leadership. In recognition of this fact, the PAP, while encouraging cultural and religious manifestations of ethnicity, has consistently suppressed expressions of communally based political dissent. For example, articulation of grievances of the Chinese-educated community by the Nanyang Siang Pau newspaper led to government intervention in 1971 (Chan 1976). Similarly, communally based economic associations have been largely ignored and bypassed in development planning. The Chinese Chamber of Commerce, for example, has been criticized by government leaders for its exclusively Chinese orientation. In addition, the government has perhaps unintentionally undercut communal social organization through systematic encouragement of English-medium over non-English-medium education, culminating, in the late 1970s, in efforts to consolidate Nanyang University with the English-medium University of Singapore in order to raise the English competence and thus employability of Nanyang University students. And the government has continued to arrest and prosecute oppositional candidates for public office who have raised "communal" issues. Following the 1976 Parliamentary elections, for instance, Ho Juan Thai, an unsuccessful Workers' Party candidate, was charged by the Home Affairs Ministry with having "played up gut issues of Chinese language, education and culture with the aim of inciting the Chinese-speaking population to violent chauvinistic reaction. . . . He repeatedly accused the government of 'killing Chinese education' when he knew the government policy had all along been to give equal treatment to all language streams" (The Straits Times 1/1/77). A second candidate, Shamsuddin Tung, was arrested on similar charges.

CONCLUSION

We may conclude this chapter, then, by suggesting that the colonial economy in general, and employment relations in particular, were organized around emergent communal bonds and loyalties, and that such bonds in turn were supported by the success of the economic enterprise they made possible. It has also been seen that labor organizations derived their early associational strength from essentially communal loyalties that later became the basis for effective opposition first to colonial and later to PAP rule. Finally, it was seen that in its efforts to consolidate political rule and enhance political stability, the PAP has demobilized both labor and its communal associational sources, a process accelerated by educational, housing, and other policies. In a later chapter, we shall explore the further impact of rapid industrialization for social organization in Singapore.

3

THE EMERGENCE
OF BUREAUCRATIC-AUTHORITARIAN
CORPORATISM IN LABOR RELATIONS

It was noted in Chapter 1 that during the 1960s many developing countries increasingly tended to establish bureaucratic-authoritarian corporatist labor relations in order to pursue goals of political stabilization and economic growth. Such corporatist strategies have typically involved, interalia, depoliticization of organized labor, wage controls, replacement of collective bargaining by government disputes-settlement procedures, drawing government sanctioned unions into officially recognized federation structures, deregistration of oppositional unions, and strong assertion of the priority of national development goals over sectional economic interests.

CORPORATISM IN SINGAPORE

In Singapore, the institutionalization of corporatist labor relations has been an especially important aspect of development planning by virtue of the fact that apart from its strategic geographical location and excellent natural harbor, Singapore's only significant development resource has been its abundant, urbanized, and economically ambitious labor force. By consequence, development planning has strongly emphasized the upgrading, utilization, and discipline of labor. On one hand, the government has made massive human capital investments in housing, education and job training, health, and public welfare, and partly on this count claims membership in the ranks of Socialist countries. But on the other hand, the government has increasingly taken steps to enhance its returns on such investments through stringent controls on union demands and labor costs.

41

By 1964 the People's Action Party had effectively depoliticized labor. This was accomplished largely through the suppression of oppositional unions and leadership in order to eliminate the organizational basis for the effective articulation of grievances vis-a-vis government elites and policy (Chan 1976). As seen in Table 3.1, an immediate consequence of this campaign against oppositional unionism was a reduction in industrial work stoppages by approximately 90 percent. Continuing moderate levels of industrial conflict up until 1968 centered mainly around economic issues (Yoshihara 1976), thus reflecting the continuing role even of politically demobilized unions in collective bargaining. On the other hand, the period 1965-68 saw the creation by the PAP of an increasingly comprehensive corporatist system of labor controls that went far beyond simply the suppression of labor, but that sought as well its incorporation into the ruling structure itself.

From the outset of PAP rule in 1959, party leaders had pledged to allow no private interest groups to sabotage official development plans for Singapore (Chan 1976, p. 36). And particularly after its expulsion from the Malaysian federation, government leaders could point to the real possibility that Singapore could not survive on its own, economically or politically, without heightened unity, discipline, and sacrifice, and that excessive demands from labor or other special interest groups could therefore threaten national survival itself. In the interest of rapid industrialization, therefore, unions had to give up their narrow membership-welfare orientation and look to their broader responsibilities to the nation: responsibilities which included wage restraint, increased productivity, and industrial discipline. To continue in their traditional role as spokesmen for strictly labor interests came to be viewed as fundamentally antisocial.

CORPORATISM IN INDUSTRIAL RELATIONS

The structural basis for Singapore's growing labor corporatism centered on the National Trades Union Congress. It will be recalled that the NTUC was created by the PAP as a progovernment alternative to the leftist union alliance under the Singapore Association of Trade Unions and subsequently became Singapore's only officially recognized labor federation. Continuing PAP control over the NTUC resulted from a number of factors. First, until the early 1970s, the NTUC was financially dependent upon government for many of its activities (Gan 1977). Its very headquarters and convention hall were built with government funds. Second, in addition to government influence over union leadership choice, there is substantial personnel overlap between the PAP and the NTUC. During 1970-73, PAP

TABLE 3.1

Number of Work Stoppages (Strikes and/or Lockouts)—
Workers Involved and Man-days Lost

Period	Stoppages	Workers Involved	Man-days Lost[a]
1946	47	50,325	845,637
1947	45	24,561	492,708
1948	20	20,585	128,657
1949	3	935	6,618
1950	1	87	4,692
1951	4	1,185	20,640
1952	5	10,067	40,105
1953	4	8,870	47,361
1954	8	11,191	135,206
1955	275	57,433	946,354
1956	29	12,373	454,455
1957	27	8,233	109,349
1958	22	2,679	78,166
1959	40	1,939	26,587
1960	45	5,939	152,005
1961	116	43,584	410,889
1962	88	6,647	165,124
1963[b]	47	33,004	388,219
1964	39	2,535	35,908
1965	30	3,374	45,800
1966	14	1,288	44,762
1967	10	4,491	41,322
1968	4	172	11,447
1969	—	—	8,512
1970	5	1,749	2,514
1971	2	1,380	5,499
1972	10	3,168	18,233
1973	5	1,312	2,295
1974	10	1,901	5,380
1975	7	1,865	4,853
1976	4	1,576	3,193
1977	—	—	1,011

[a]Figures relate to man-days lost within the period shown, irrespective of whether or not the stoppages began in that period or earlier.

[b]Figures include the two-day general strike in October involving approximately 19,700 workers and 34,300 man-days lost.

Source: Ministry of Labour.

Members of Parliament occupied seven of the seats of the NTUC Central Committee and provided top-level executive leadership in some of the larger affiliate national unions as well. In 1977, 15 Members of Parliament, including a senior parliamentary secretary and three parliamentary secretaries, were active in union affairs as resource persons and advisors.

Further PAP guidance of union activities is effected through the NTUC Research Unit. This government-supported unit plays an important advisory role in the formulation of union bargaining claims and strategies (Chalmers and Pang 1969).

Growing PAP control of NTUC and national union leadership and policy was accompanied by consolidation and centralization of the union structure itself. In part, such consolidation is based on the multiple leadership roles of top union officials. Until 1980, for example, Phey Yew Kok was not only a member of Parliament, NTUC president, and executive secretary of the NTUC Industrial Affairs Council, but in addition he was secretary-general of two major unions, the Singapore Industrial Labour Organization and the Pioneer Industries Employees' Union, and president of a third, the Singapore Air Transport Union (The Straits Times 12/16/76).

By the late 1960s, the NTUC had effectively established its authority over affiliate unions in all questions of policy relating to government, general economic and national matters, union organizational structure, internal discipline, and organizational growth (Chalmers 1967; Chalmers and Pang 1969). The national headquarters of affiliated unions made decisions regarding bargaining strategies and issues within the parameters established at the federation level and with the assistance of the Research Unit. These decisions, made at national union headquarters, in turn guided local branches (Chalmers and Pang 1969). Illustrative of NTUC control over local bargaining was the requirement announced in 1974 that all union negotiating claims had to be submitted for approval by the NTUC disputes committee before being introduced into contract negotiations (The Straits Times 12/24/74).

The NTUC has been the major instrumentality through which labor has assumed a productionist role in national development, a role which has emphasized the needs for stabilization of labor costs, increased labor productivity, and industrial peace. Labor's national developmental mandate was described in 1976 by Labour Minister Ong Pang Boon in the following terms:

> Singaporeans, led by a responsible and disciplined
> union movement, [have] demonstrated their resolve
> and ability, despite economic uncertainties, in main-
> taining industrial stability and successfully building

up a strong and viable economy. . . . These same
qualities [are] needed for the task ahead: responsible
and constructive unionism, hard work, the willingness
to learn better skills and acquire new ones, the ready
appreciation of the economic problems confronting
them, and the strength to sacrifice personal interests
for the national good (The Straits Times 5/1/76).

Later the same year, Minister Ong urged the NTUC to explain
to workers the need for greater moderation in demands for wage increases and fringe benefits, while the Economic Development Board
asked the NTUC to help reduce "job-hopping" in order to strengthen
Singapore's competitive export position vis-a-vis Korea, Taiwan,
and Hong Kong (The Straits Times 10/30/76).

The NTUC leadership has accepted its new productionist role
with enthusiasm. Formal assumption of such a role was symbolized
in the 1965 ratification by the NTUC, Singapore Manufacturers' Association, and the Singapore Federation of a "Charter for Industrial
Progress," under which labor agreed to work jointly with management toward the shared goals of increased productivity and industrial
peace. The more tangible expression of this role, however, is seen
in the active attempts by union officials, particularly since 1968, to
urge wage restraint and greater work discipline among workers.
For example, following a protracted period of decline in foreign investment during the 1974-75 recession, Devan Nair, NTUC secretary-
general, suggested that:

our working population may well have to undergo a
period of belt-tightening all round. . . . it is clear
that an essential element in our new strategy must be
a tighter grip on wage increases. . . . if we do not
quickly and willingly change to low gear on the wages
front, we shall further discourage investment and
aggravate the unemployment problem (The Straits Times
2/29/76).

The following month the rationale for such wage constraint
was further amplified by Lawrence Sia, another prominent NTUC
official. "Good unionists," he said, should "play their role in economic development by providing favourable conditions to attract investments from multinationals. . . ." Thus, unions needed leaders
"with enough strength to prevent any action that would kill the goose
that lays the golden egg" (The Straits Times 3/23/76). The next
month leaders of the two largest NTUC affiliates came out in support of wage restraint (The Straits Times 4/28/76). Immediately

after that, the NTUC asked members of these unions to refrain, as well, from making further demands for improved fringe benefits, a request agreed to by union leaders the same day (The Straits Times 4/30/76). Thereafter, for several months, the NTUC newspaper continued to urge workers to accept smaller wage increments in line with National Wages Council* recommendations.

The disciplinary role of the NTUC became especially clear during 1974-75 when shrinking employment opportunities and lack of wage increases led to increasing labor dissatisfaction and protest. In a speech delivered in late 1974, Nair warned of:

> the usual crop of adventurers who will feel tempted to try their luck with the workers of Singapore [when times become hard]. . . . They will have the day-lights whacked out of them, and with the overwhelming endorsement of the trade union movement and of public opinion generally (The Straits Times 11/3/74).

The following month an official in the Singapore Manual and Mercantile Workers Union, one of the largest NTUC affiliates, warned against irresponsible wage demands, and cautioned "adventurers and desperadoes not to pour oil into troubled waters," saying the union "would not hesitate to act against such antisocial elements" (The Straits Times 12/24/74). At about the same time, the union initiated an inquiry into a strike by an affiliate branch at the Interocean Company and issued a strong statement against the strike (The Straits Times 5/25/75) while the labor Ministry and police began official inquiries. Following these union attacks and government inquiries, the branch officials involved in the strike resigned (The Straits Times 8/14/75).

The productionist role of the NTUC is further brought out in its strong involvement in efforts to raise productivity. Following the 1975 launching of a National Productivity Campaign by Singapore's National Productivity Board, Devan Nair asserted that "It is only the moral authority of the NTUC leadership which persuades the rank-and-file to give our initiates in the field of launching productivity councils . . . a fair trial" (Sunday Nation 3/23/75).

The following month NTUC President Phey Yew Kok pledged his support of the campaign: "The National Trades Union Congress has already given—and will continue to give—its wholehearted support to all endeavours aimed at raising productivity" (The Straits Times 4/12/75).

---

*The National Wages Council is discussed below.

The concrete forms such support has taken include continuing efforts to reduce high labor force turnover rates and assist in government efforts to introduce productivity incentive programs such as the 1978 "merit-demerit" wage scheme in industry (The Straits Times 7/22/78).

Increasing corporatism in the trade union structure has been accompanied by corporatism in industrial relations as well. Between 1965 and 1968, although the NTUC was increasingly centralized and drawn into a close relationship with PAP leadership, unions continued to act essentially as interest groups engaged in collective bargaining for the pursuit of sectoral economic gains. As late as 1967, Chalmers (1967) was still able to argue that collective bargaining was more important than legislation, administrative action, or the decisions of national arbitration courts in determining employment relations in Singapore. Indicative of the lack of substantive regulation of employment relations by government was the absence of an income policy and a tendency for the Industrial Arbitration Court, established under a 1960 Ordinance, to base its decisions less on the state of the economy than on considerations of power, equity, and ability to pay on the part of disputants themselves (Chalmers 1967, p. 93).

All this was to change in 1968 with the passage of two new pieces of labor legislation which are considered by some to be among the toughest outside the communist world (Yoshihara 1976). The first of these, The Employment Act, addressed the commonly recognized problem of steadily rising labor costs based on collective bargaining (Chalmers 1967) by reducing permissible retrenchment benefits, overtime work, bonuses, maternity and holiday leave, and fringe benefits. While the act left actual wage determination to collective bargaining, it did slow the rapid increase in nonwage remuneration. The second piece of legislation, the Industrial Relations Act, was even more important in reducing the importance of collective bargaining in Singapore, for this act gave management full discretionary power in matters of promotion, transfer, recruitment, dismissal, reinstatement, assignment or allocation of duties, and termination by reasons of reorganization or redundancy. All these functions were now entirely excluded from negotiation. And indicative of labor's acceptance of its new productionist role was the absence of a single negative vote, even on the part of labor M.P.s, when the new legislation was presented to Parliament (Chan 1976).

The 1968 downgrading of collective bargaining in favor of legislative and managerial determination of employment relations supplemented and consolidated an already existing system of administrative conciliation and arbitration. Disputes which cannot readily be resolved through private collective bargaining must be submitted for conciliation through the Ministry of Labor. Where such conciliation is unsuccessful, the Labor Minister or either of the disputants may submit the case to the Industrial Arbitration Court (IAC) for settlement. Rulings of the IAC are final and may not be appealed further. The IAC also plays an important role in certification of collective agreements, a role which ensures compliance with legal provisions of employment legislation. It may be noted in connection with Singapore's increasingly corporatist industrial relations system that, whereas formerly the IAC arrived at decisions with little regard to national economic or policy implications of particular settlements, the court has more recently moved toward a greater concern for the broader ramifications of collective agreements for national economic development (Seminar Delegates 1977).

The cumulative effect of existing labor legislation and the new 1968 laws on industrial relations in Singapore is evident in a second major decline in work stoppages during 1968-69 (Table 3.1). It should be noted that whereas the earlier decline in 1964 was a consequence of the depoliticization of organized labor, this second decline resulted from the elaboration of a corporatist system which substantially reduced the role of economic bargaining and conflict in employment relations, replacing it with substantive regulation by the state. Pang and Tan (1972) have summarized the legal and political factors which explain Singapore's remarkable lack of industrial conflict since 1968:

> The entire legal framework is constructed to ensure industrial peace. Unions may only be formed under carefully stipulated rules. Their registration is at the discretion of the Labour Minister. The Government may deregister any union without stating reasons or having to justify the action in a court of law. The Industrial Relations Act provides that an industrial dispute may not proceed further if the Industrial Arbitration Court has taken cognizance of it. Such a provision virtually ensures that compulsory or voluntary arbitration will be resorted to. In practice any strike which does not have the direct or indirect sympathy of the Labour Ministry is unlikely to occur (p. 131). . . . Foreign companies will not be threatened with arbitrary and capricious action. Disruptive strikes and labour unrest will not be tolerated, and all the state powers will be marshalled to forestall their appearance (p. 133).

While the corporatist system was essentially in place by 1968, subsequent legislative and organizational changes have further

extended it. It was noted earlier that Singapore formerly lacked a
wages or incomes policy and that unions retained a collective bargaining role in this area even under the restrictive 1968 legislation.
But after 1972 wage issues, too, were largely removed from the
province of collective bargaining through the creation of a National
Wages Council. This advisory wages board, composed of representatives of government, labor (NTUC), and employers, meets on
a yearly basis to:

a. formulate general guidelines on wages,
b. recommend necessary adjustments in wage structure, with a
   view to developing a coherent wage system consistent with long-
   term economic and social development, and
c. help devise incentive schemes to improve operational efficiency
   and productivity (Pang and Kay 1974, p. 19).

This council, which "underscores the centralized guidance
that the party government gives to the industrial relations system"
(Pang and Kay 1974, p. 20) is now an important component of a
national incomes policy and provides wage guidelines, subject to
government approval, for union-management negotiations and IAC
rulings.

Authoritarian corporatism is by necessity a patrimonial system in which interest groups exist and interact with the state solely
at the discretion of the ruling elite. In Singapore's political context,
lobbying and interest representation before government are shaped
by a new "political culture which discourages conflict, confronta-
tion, and bargaining, and emphasizes stability, low risk and petition. Responses . . . are at the largess of the ruling leadership
. . . [which] . . . has to be wise, efficient, and just" (Chan 1976,
p. 43).

Patrimonial discretion is a necessary basis for corporatist
control in Singapore. First and of great importance is the absolute
power of the Registrar of Trade Unions to register and deregister
unions without justification (Tan Boon Chiang 1973). Second, given
the relative bargaining weakness of organized labor, initially because of labor abundance and more recently because of increasingly
restrictive labor legislation, labor very much needs the backing of
government in its dealings with employers. Without the sympathetic
ear of the Minister of Labour, unions are unlikely to deal successfully with management. Nair has recognized the importance of Min-
isterial protection of labor interests in the context of legislatively
backed managerial power. After pointing to numerous cases in
which the Ministry of Labour had intervened on behalf of workers
regarding unfair dismissals and other cases of worker victimization,

he concluded that: "It is vital to the maintenance of industrial peace and stability in Singapore that the Labour Ministry continue to monitor and investigate very closely allegations relating to the abuse of management prerogatives" (Sunday Times 10/9/77).

Illustrative of the weak position of unions which lack government support or sympathy is the case of the Metal Workers' Union, a non-NTUC affiliated house union of the British Metal Box Company, during their 1977 strike. This was the only strike recorded in Singapore that year. Metal Box workers had protested management's refusal to give them a half day off for Chinese New Year. When management fired 22 workers in connection with this dispute, the other workers downed tools and demanded the dismissal of the Personnel Manager responsible for the firings. When management retaliated again by firing more workers, union officials approached the Ministry of Labour for assistance but were refused a hearing on the grounds that the strike was illegal since the demand for the removal of a personnel manager or reinstatement of fired workers violated legislative provision that, in personnel matters, management prerogative could not be challenged by workers. Subsequently, the union lost worker support and an NTUC affiliate stepped in and was quickly recognized as the new representative of Metal Box Workers. The old Metal Box Workers Union was formally deregistered.

In order to reduce the subsequent likelihood of such disruptions, Parliament passed a bill authorizing the Ministry of Labour to freeze the bank account of any union under investigation by the Ministry or the Registrar of Unions (The Straits Times 3/24/77).

CORPORATE STABILITY IN SINGAPORE

Singapore's bureaucratic-authoritarian corporatism has proven remarkably durable by comparison with similar experiments in several other countries. In order to understand the sources of such stability, it is useful to refer back to the earlier enumerated social conditions supportive of authoritarian corporatism. First, following the PAP purge of party and union leftists, the ruling elite has been highly cohesive, with few serious disaffections or conflicts. In her study of Singapore politics, Chan Heng Chee concluded that: "the amazing elite cohesion of the present PAP leadership must to a great extent be attributed to their experience in fighting and maneuvering against common enemies, first the colonial authorities, but more so in the intra-party struggle [of the early 1960s . . . in addition] there are some members who are primarily technocrats, who see their contribution more in expertise than as a politician" (1975, p. 61).

Second, the local bourgeoisie lacks the stature or resource base to challenge PAP rule. In part this follows from relative domestic economic stagnation during the 1960s which slowed the emergence of a viable, strong, and independent local bourgeoisie. Third, through corporatist controls over existing social and economic groups and political demobilization of others, the PAP has effectively atomized nonincorporated popular sectors of society and thus eliminated the organizational basis for independent grievance or demand formulation. Such atomization outside corporatist structures is reflected in the fact that by 1977, only 7 percent of all unionized employees belonged to unions not affiliated with the NTUC (Ong, quoted in The Straits Times 3/24/77).

Finally, through government control of radio and television broadcasting (Kuo 1978) and controls over other mass media, the government has gained control of most public communication. In addition, it restricts and censors foreign magazines and films and goes to great lengths to filter, evaluate, criticize, and interpret incoming news for the local readership.

CONCLUSION

During the early 1960s, the PAP was mainly preoccupied with problems of demobilizing leftist opposition. After the 1965 expulsion from the Malaysian federation, party priorities shifted to problems of economic survival and growth. And, given the centrality of labor in industrialization policy planning, a major effort was made to harness labor to development goals through the establishment of corporatist state-union controls. Growing corporatism was reflected in the reorganization and subordination of labor, the displacement of bargaining and conflict by legislative, administrative, and judicial determination of employment relations, enhancement of managerial authority, and, later, institutionalization of an incomes policy. In the next chapter, we describe the rapid post-1968 industrialization which in part resulted from corporatist labor controls.

4

SINGAPORE'S POST-1965
INDUSTRIAL TRANSFORMATION

Chapter 3 described the emergence of corporatist state-union relations culminating in the 1968 labor legislation. This chapter will discuss the rapid industrialization that was stimulated by this and other legislative and institutional changes during the late 1960s and that was characterized by a disproportionate growth in foreign and state enterprise and relative stagnation in domestic enterprise. In Chapter 5 we will discuss the social impact of such a development pattern, as well as its implications for authoritarian corporatism.

EARLY INDUSTRIALIZATION POLICY:
RATIONALE AND IMPLEMENTATION

From the very beginning of PAP rule in 1959, it was clear that Singapore's economic growth would have to be based on rapid industrialization in order to generate employment for a growing labor force. A highly influential United Nations report, published in 1961, estimated a need for 214,000 new jobs between 1961 and 1970 in order to achieve full employment and argued that entrepot trade could be expected to provide no more than a total 116,000 of these jobs (Goh 1969, p. 128). Anticipation of stagnation in entrepot trade, the traditional backbone of the economy, was based on recognition that neighboring countries were establishing direct trade with other countries and thus bypassing Singapore (Lee 1976, p. 6).

In order to encourage rapid industrialization, the People's Action Party enacted a number of laws to attract new investment. Especially important was the Pioneer Industries (Relief from Income Tax) Ordinance No. 1 that reduced the tax rate from 40 percent to only 4 percent for a five-year period for companies that qualified as "pioneer industries." A second ordinance, the Industrial Expansion (Relief from Income Tax) Ordinance No. 2, reduced taxes for firms that expanded in order to produce approved products. These and other legislative acts were intended largely to encourage the creation and expansion of local manufacturing firms, although they did not discriminate against foreign investors. They have been followed by other laws such as the 1967 Economic Expansion Act that further increased the scope of incentives for industrial investment and a 1975 extension of pioneer industries tax relief to ten years. In addition, and at the recommendation of the 1961 UN mission report, the government established an Economic Development Board (EDB) both to implement the government's industrialization plans and to be the instrument of the government's direct participation in the economy. Until 1968 the EDB was responsible for industrial estate development and loans, assistance to new investors, and the handling of applications for loans, pioneer status, and tariff protection.

Prior to 1968 industrial investment was associated with rapid growth in national income but had little effect on unemployment. This was in part a result of growing foreign investment in such capital-intensive industries as chemicals and petroleum, basic metals, and engineering. By far the most important of these was the petroleum industry (see Table 4.1), whose growth was based on a need for oil refining facilities closer to the rapidly growing economies of the Asian Pacific region. Between 1963 and 1968, the percentage of total industrial value-added accounted for by chemical and petroleum products increased from 15 percent to 23 percent (Lee Soo Ann 1973, p. 79). On the other hand, this industrial group employed only 6 percent of the labor force in 1963 and 5 percent in 1968, thus indicating its high capital intensity. Another rapidly growing industry during this period was transport equipment, especially shipbuilding. Shipbuilding and repair, along with textiles and wood and cork, were in fact the only significant contributors to manufacturing employment growth between 1963 and 1968, as seen in Table 4.1.

CONTINUING EMPLOYMENT PROBLEMS AND
NEW POLICY INITIATIVES IN THE
POSTSEPARATION PERIOD

Continuing capital-intensive industrialization in the context of an increasingly stagnant entrepot economy and rapid population growth was associated with growing unemployment during the 1960s (Oshima 1968). This problem was heightened in 1965 by the separa-

TABLE 4.1

Industrial Value-Added and Employment in Selected Years

Industry	Value-Added (millions of dollars)				Employment (thousands)			
	1963	1965	1968	1970	1963	1965	1968	1970
Food manufacturing	20	32	62	76	5	5	7	9
Beverages	23	27	30	35	2	2	2	2
Tobacco	19	27	29	25	1	1	1	1
Textiles, footwear and leather	5	13	22	56	2	6	13	20
Wood and cork	14	19	43	61	3	5	7	9
Furniture and fixtures	5	5	9	11	1	1	2	2
Paper and paper products	2	4	9	13	1	1	3	3
Printing and publishing	30	35	37	51	5	5	5	7
Rubber products	4	7	15	32	1	1	2	4
Chemicals, chemical and petroleum products	39	60	139	260	2	2	4	6
Nonmetallic mineral products	25	24	28	33	3	3	3	5
Basic metal products	5	11	22	22	—	1	2	2
Metal products	20	30	46	72	3	4	6	9
Machinery	7	9	18	28	1	1	3	4
Electrical machinery	10	11	17	128	1	2	2	13
Transport equipment	20	26	64	159	4	5	8	16
Miscellaneous	5	9	22	32	2	2	5	9
Totals	253	349	612	1,094	37	47	75	121

Source: Lee Soo Ann 1973, pp. 79–80

tion of Singapore from Malaysia. Prior to the separation, government had encouraged local consumer goods industries through protective tariffs and financial assistance. Such domestic market oriented industry was seriously hurt by the separation and by the consequent loss of a large domestic market following the erection of trade barriers between Singapore and Malaysia (Lee Soo Ann 1973). To add to these difficulties, the British Labour Government, in 1966, announced its intention to withdraw all British military forces from Singapore by 1971. Since the British bases employed approximately 40,000 workers, the withdrawal was expected to further exacerbate unemployment problems.

Given the recognition that serious and chronic unemployment might precipitate political instability (Snow 1980, p. 20) and endanger the very survival of an independent Singapore, the PAP moved toward a policy of rapid industrialization based in large measure on the attraction of foreign investment into export oriented, labor-intensive industry. The desire to increase foreign industrial investment had been initially suggested in the 1961 UN report, where it was argued that:

> Singapore will have to supplement on a comparatively
> large scale during the initial period its own resources
> . . . with those from abroad. . . . For this reason,
> the necessity of attracting foreign co-operation on a
> large scale should be recognized . . . (quoted in Tan
> 1979).

In particular, it was felt that following the separation from Malaysia industrialization would have to be based primarily on export oriented manufacturing and that, in the short run at least, only large international firms possessed the requisite technological and market capacities to successfully compete in world markets. Thus, while there was no desire to exclude domestic private enterprise from industrial participation, neither was there to be any special protection or favor accorded local over foreign investors. In its investment promotion activities, the Economic Development Board established services not only for local investors but also set up overseas offices and promotional centers in the United States and Europe, organized trade fairs and exhibitions, and provided information, tours, and other special assistance to potential overseas investors.

In order to reduce unemployment, special priority was accorded labor-intensive industries. And the special sensitivity of such investment to industrial conflict and relative labor costs provided the central rationale for the corporalist labor legislation introduced during the late 1960s. As late as 1976, and despite stringent labor controls and an effective wage policy, T. Isobe, president of Singapore's Japanese Chamber of Commerce and Industry, warned of the continuing need to hold down labor costs:

> There are . . . certain barriers to foreign investment in Singapore. Firstly, Singapore's domestic market is small. Japanese investors will have to be attracted to Singapore on the competitiveness of her export oriented industries. And the biggest deterrent to international competitiveness is labour cost. Although a potential investor does not consider only labour costs, but weighs the entire cost-package, it is still true that high wages often unbalance other costs (quoted in Business Times 1976).

In recognition of the importance of skill levels and worker productivity in reducing labor costs, the government also made substantial investments in basic vocational and industrial training. By the early 1970s, the government was involved in extensive industrial training programs through the EDB and an Industrial Training Board, secondary school vocational education, cooperative training schemes with private industry, and direct EDB training assistance to firms needing particular categories of skills (Asian Business and Industry 12/76, p. 43).

The centrality of government efforts to control labor costs in the total package of "incentives" for foreign investment was made clear in a recent statement by Minister of Labour Ong Pang Boon. In 1977, Ong argued that all the elements for a good manufacturing center could be found in Singapore:

> The location is strategic, the infrastructure developed, and the services efficient. Our unions are responsible, our workers willing, and our wages competitive. Foreign investors who bring with them the technology and the markets will find the Republic a profitable place to set up their factories (The Straits Times 4/1/77).

THE POST-1968 INDUSTRIAL TRANSFORMATION

Between 1967 and 1977 Singapore's capital income more than tripled while unemployment rates were cut in half (Department of Statistics 1978). In 1977 Singapore was officially removed from the UN roster of "developing societies" eligible for concessionary interest rates on international loans and for special UN development assistance. This economic transformation was based in part on continued expansion in industries which had been important before 1968 and in part on new government economic ventures. But in large measure, Singapore's success in solving its most pressing problem, that of unemployment, has centered on the massive inflow of foreign capital into electronics and other labor-absorbing, export oriented industries.

While local manufacturing had been severely hurt by the separation from Malaysia, other traditional trade and finance related businesses have continued to play a significant, if shrinking, role in Singapore s economy. Particularly important has been the domestic banking industry that has grown and prospered as a result of Singapore's general economic expansion. Similarly dynamic have been tourism-related services, real estate and housing, and, within the manufacturing sector, food and beverages, transportation, and some service and supply industries linked to foreign industry.

In addition, some of the newer and largely foreign manufacturing industries which led the pre-1968 industrial expansion have remained important. In particular, textiles, petroleum, and transport equipment industries have continued to grow.

The third element in Singapore's rapid growth has been state enterprise, often in the form of joint ventures with foreign investors. The government holds approximately one-third of net fixed assets in 12 principal industrial categories (Far Eastern Economic Review 10/28/77). In 1977, through the Ministry of Finance and its holding company, Temasek, the government held controlling interests in some 70 companies. It also held partial or complete control over many other companies through INTRACO, a government trading company, and through the Development Bank of Singapore, which is 49 percent government owned. All told, the government controlled assets of approximately $1 billion (The Straits Times 2/16/77) in such varied industries as shipping, trading, banking and finance, air transport, oil servicing and transport, shipbuilding and repair, iron and steel, petroleum refining, food and beverage manufacturing, footwear, textiles, lumber, printing, and industrial chemicals (Shaw, Chen, Lee, and Thomson 1977, pp. 109-16).

Particularly significant has been government investment in shipyards. Such investment was initially based on a desire to counter the anticipated unemployment created by the British military pullout by converting old naval bases into commercial shipyards. One of the largest such yards, Jurong Shipyard, is a joint venture with IHI, a Japanese firm.

While the government is the single most important entrepreneur in the Singapore economy (Tan 1975), it, along with other domestic investors, has played a relatively minor overall role in the Republic's post-1968 industrial transformation. In 1972, for example, 84 percent of government equity in wholly owned companies was confined to only three companies, one of which was Neptune Orient Lines, the national maritime fleet (Tan 1975). Far more important has been foreign capital investment in banking, oil exploration and refining, shipbuilding and repair, and labor-intensive industry. Total foreign manufacturing investment now outweighs state manufacturing investment by a factor of more than ten to one (Far Eastern Economic Review 10/28/77).

Prior to the late 1960s, Singapore's banking industry was dominated by a few large Chinese banks and two major colonial era banks, The Chartered Bank and The Hongkong and Shanghai Bank. Much of the recent growth in banking, however, is attributable to the involvement of such large foreign banks as Bank of America, Chase-Manhattan, and Citibank in the Singapore-based Asia dollar market. The extent of foreign penetration of the banking industry is suggested by the fact that in 1970, 11 out of 37, or 30 percent, of the registered banks (excluding representative offices) were domestically owned, whereas only 13 out of 70, or 19 percent, were domestically owned in 1975 (Price and Waterhouse 1976). Similarly, petroleum exploration and refining have been entirely foreign dominated, while four of the seven major shipyards are Japanese majority owned.

As noted earlier, with the exception of shipbuilding and repair, all these industries provided a basis for rapid growth in national income but had little effect on unemployment. It was only after passage of the 1968 labor legislation that new foreign investments began to have a substantial employment impact. As seen in Table 4.1, the greatest percentage increases in both value-added and employment between 1968 and 1970 were in such labor-absorbing manufacturing industries as textiles, footwear and leather, transport equipment, and electrical machinery. By 1977, electronics alone accounted for 15 percent of Singapore's total manufacturing output and a much larger percent of industrial employment. It was largely these industries which explain the near doubling of manufacturing output and employment* shown in Table 4.2 between 1968 and 1971. The importance of the 1968 legislation for such investment was explicitly recognized by Foreign Minister Rajaratnam in his

---

*The substantially lower capital intensity of the rapidly growing new textile, electronics, and other industries is suggested by Table 4.3, which shows the value of fixed capital per worker by industry in 1970.

observation in 1970 that the new labor laws were directly responsible for an increase of $165 million in investment and a resultant addition of 35,000 jobs between 1968 and 1970 (The Straits Times 11/23/70).

TABLE 4.2

Indicators of Industrial Expansion, 1963-74

Year	Output (million dollars)	Number of Workers
1963	844	36,586
1964	928	41,488
1965	1,086	47,334
1966	1,326	52,807
1967	1,687	58,347
1968	2,176	74,833
1969	3,214	100,758
1970	3,891	120,509
1971	4,699	140,552
1972	5,722	170,352
1973	7,938	198,574
1974	13,347	206,607

Source: Adapted from Singapore International Chamber of Commerce, Investor's Guide, July 1976, p. 60.

Most of the new manufacturing investment was export oriented, as shown by the fact that by 1976, 59 percent of Singapore's total manufacturing output was exported (The Straits Times 2/8/77), as against only 32.5 percent in 1965 (S. A. Lee 1973). And approximately 85 percent of total exports was from foreign or foreign majority owned firms (Tan, 1978).

The overwhelming role of foreign capital in this post-1968 industrialization is equally clear. Between 1968 and 1969, foreign manufacturing investment rose from $184 million (U.S.) to $515 million (Buchanan 1969), followed by further substantial increases during the 1970s (see Table 4.4).

It has been estimated that by the early 1970s, over one-half of total investment stock in banking and manufacturing (Lee Soo Ann 1977) and 45 percent of manufacturing employment was accounted for by foreign firms (Pang and Tan 1972). Such strong foreign participation was especially pronounced in the new labor-absorbing industries. Of 63 textile firms registered in 1972, 60 were foreign majority owned. In electronics, while 12 of the 58 electronics firms were domestic, most were small and few were in technologically sophisticated phases of the industry (Pang and Lim 1972). As of 1977, there was only one large, technologically advanced domestic firm, the Industrial Electronics and Engineering Ltd. The other large local electronics firm, Setron, Ltd., is in fact a joint venture with Sony (Asian Wall Street Journal 12/14/77).

TABLE 4.3

Fixed Capital Per Worker by Industry, 1970

Industry	Value (Singapore dollars)
Food	$5,700
Beverage	8,000
Tobacco	7,000
Textiles, footwear, and leather	3,000
Wood and cork	4,000
Furniture and fixtures	900
Paper and paper products	2,100
Printing and publishing	4,300
Rubber products	5,500
Chemicals, chemical and petroleum products	47,400
Nonmetallic minerals	5,200
Basic metal	9,800
Metal products	3,700
Machinery	1,900
Electrical machinery	1,400
Transport equipment	2,300
Miscellaneous manufacturing	1,100
Average value for all industries	5,500

Source: Adapted from Lee 1973, p. 85.

The relative economic stagnation of domestic firms in contrast to the recent rapid expansion in foreign enterprise is best brought out by changes in several indicators of the relative shares of local and foreign firms. Between 1966 and 1975, the percentage

TABLE 4.4

Foreign Investment in Singapore Manufacturing Industries
by Country of Origin as at End of 1970–75 (Actual)
(in terms of gross fixed assets)
(million Singapore dollars)

	1970	1971	1972	1973	1974	1975	1976	1977
United States	343	501	840	992	1,082	1,118	1,233	
Japan	68	108	137	237	354	454	525	
European Economic								
Community	406	616	863	912	997	1,112	1,241	
United Kingdom	119	294	375	390	424	481	555	
Netherlands	183	275	356	381	420	473	524	
West Germany	3	21	96	102	107	107	115	
France	8	10	15	17	21	22	18	
Italy	10	12	15	15	15	15	16	
Denmark	3	4	6	7	10	12	11	
Others—ECC	—	—	—	—	—	2	2	
Others	178	350	443	518	621	696	740	
Total	995	1,575	2,283	2,659	3,054	3,380	3,739	4,145

Source: Economic Development Board.

of manufacturing employment generated by foreign or foreign majority owned firms increased from 25 percent to 52 percent. By 1979
wholly foreign owned firms alone accounted for 63 percent of total
industrial employment (Wong, cited in Snow 1980, p. 20). Similarly, industrial output between 1966 and 1972 increased 2.7 times
for domestic firms, 3.7 times for local majority owned firms, 3
times among majority foreign owned firms, and 7.9 times for wholly
foreign owned firms (Yoshihara 1976). In 1975, multinational corporations in the manufacturing sector absorbed 76 percent of manufacturing inputs, produced 71 percent of outputs, and accounted for
65 percent of manufacturing capital formation.

Further evidence of the overwhelming dominance of foreign
capital in industry comes from a survey of 576 industrial firms
taken in 1974 (Yoshihara 1976). Table 4.5 shows for each of the
major industries in Singapore the percentage of paid-up capital
which was foreign in the years 1959 and 1973. The table shows a
dramatic increase in foreign participation for most industrial categories, as well as an overall increase in the percentage share of
foreign paid-up capital, from 22 percent in 1959 to 76 percent in
1973. Further suggestive of the change in the relative roles of foreign and local manufacturing investment after 1973 is data (Table 4.5)
showing that the domestic percentage of total manufacturing investment has not exceeded 34 percent, and declined to 9.4 percent in
1977.

THE DOMINANCE OF FOREIGN INDUSTRY:
SOME EXPLANATIONS

The overwhelming significance of foreign investment in Singapore's recent industrialization, despite an abundance of accumulated
local capital (Chia 1971), may be attributed to a number of factors
relating to characteristics of local industry, government industrialization policy, the superior export position of foreign firms, and the
nature of the linkage between foreign and local enterprise.

As noted earlier, the break with Malaysia led to a sudden
shrinkage of the market for local consumer goods and thus severely
damaged many of the domestic industries that had been encouraged
under the government's import substitution industrialization strategy.
There has also been a continuing tendency for local capital to flow
mainly into tertiary activities such as tourism, real estate, stock
market investment, banking, finance, and domestic trade, in part
because of uncertainties regarding Singapore's political future and a
resulting desire to maintain highly liquid assets (Hoselitz 1960, p.
152). In addition, continuing family control over local business

TABLE 4.5

Foreign Paid-up Capital in Industry, 1959 and 1973

	Total Paid-up Capital (thousand dollars)	Paid-up Capital in Foreign Controlled Firms (thousand dollars)	Percentage Foreign
		1959	
Food, beverages, tobacco	81,222	10,964	13
Textiles	3,490	1,863	53
Chemicals	8,525	3,577	19
Petroleum and petroleum products	—	—	—
Metals	26,566	14,275	54
Machinery and equipment	12,672	5,397	43
Electrical products	7,372	7,010	95
Scientific and photographic equipment	1,405	869	62
Others	111,451	12,139	11
Total	252,703	54,129	21
		1973	
Food, beverages, tobacco	242,451	126,728	52
Textiles	178,757	158,362	89
Chemicals	153,154	127,981	84
Petroleum and petroleum products	303,369	303,369	100
Metals	148,970	75,534	51
Machinery and equipment	160,681	78,036	49
Electrical products	132,194	97,753	74
Scientific and photographic equipment	64,395	60,400	94
Others	236,864	196,726	83
Total	1,620,835	1,224,889	76

Source: Adapted from Kunio Yoshihara, Foreign Investment and Domestic Response, 1976, pp. 221-22.

establishments has been associated with conservative investment attitudes and unwillingness to expand the equity base of firms by bringing in outside capital.

While government industrial policy has not explicitly favored foreign over local investors, it has nevertheless had this effect. The initial government rationale for encouraging foreign investment was based on a perception that only they possessed the technological and market capabilities for rapid, export-based industrialization. Once this policy decision was made, legislative, infrastructural, political, and financial incentives and decisions followed which had the unintended effect not only of attracting foreign investment but of ensuring its subsequent dominance over local investment as well.

First, government industrial incentives have largely favored the growth of foreign, rather than domestic, industry. Major tax incentives were offered to designated pioneer enterprises with investments of over $1 million in high priority, export oriented industries. Such incentives, which clearly favored large foreign investors, partly explain the disproportionate growth of foreign firms among pioneer industries. By 1973, only 22 percent of the firms which had qualified for pioneer status were locally owned, and these provided only 16 percent of paid-up capital among pioneer enterprises (Yoshihara 1976). This meant that it was primarily foreign firms that benefited from the substantial tax relief offered pioneer firms (Asian Wall Street Journal 12/14/77).

In addition, government provision of industrial infrastructure may often undercut small local enterprise, rather than encourage its development. The clearing of land for the creation of modern industrial estates is an excellent example of this problem. Such clearing has displaced many marginal firms which have been unable to relocate to the new estates where rental, utility, and other costs are higher and industrial regulations more strictly enforced (Gamer 1971). While such firms, left unaided, would hardly have provided a viable basis for industrialization, a policy which would have given such firms as much assistance as was in fact given the larger multinational firms might have placed local firms on a far stronger footing in Singapore's economy.

Third, the Economic Development Board, the major government instrumentality for investment promotion, has concentrated primarily on the attraction of foreign investors. Through both official and informal channels, continuing contacts between the EDB and established foreign firms are maintained in order to facilitate further expansion, diversification, and technological upgrading. By contrast, until quite recently, local promotional activities were carried out by a local-industries desk staffed by only one person and by a joint ventures bureau through which contacts between local and foreign investors were arranged.

Finally, the special access of foreign management to government assistance is amplified by their substantial local representation in government decision making. For example, the Singapore Employers' Federation, a heavily foreign dominated business association, nominates representatives to sit on the National Wages Council (NWC) and a number of public bodies. The importance of government sensitivity to the needs of foreign investors is especially clear in the case of the NWC. This body, whose purpose it is to ensure orderly wage increments and a rationalized wage structure, was initially proposed and supported by foreign companies (I. T. Tan 1972). On several occasions, the NWC has suggested that its recommended yearly wage increases be waived for export oriented firms encountering stiff overseas competition.

Another important aspect of government development policy that has had a negative impact on local entrepreneurship has been occasional direct economic competition from government enterprise. Such competition has been especially acute in banking and construction. Both local and foreign banks have noted the sometimes unfair competition by the Development Bank of Singapore, which is not subject to the limits on the type, size, and security of loans imposed on private-sector banks. Similarly, the Post Office Savings Bank can offer tax-exempt interest to savings depositors, an offering unavailable to private banks (Far Eastern Economic Review 10/18/77, pp. 36–37).

While government competition in banking is of too recent an origin to have seriously affected local enterprise, the government role in housing construction is of longer duration and greater consequence. Because of its access to government land and financial resources, government housing authorities can build housing units for sale at far lower prices than can private builders (Far Eastern Economic Review 10/28/77, p. 37). Similarly, other government enterprises can obtain concessionary interest rates on loans, monopoly control over major markets, and sometimes cheaper rates for public services such as utilities and warehousing.

The Chinese business community has long recognized government, rather than foreign enterprise, as its chief competitor in the local economy, and in 1977 the Chinese Chamber of Commerce appealed for tax incentives for local business similar to those offered pioneer (usually foreign) firms, while also registering an indirect complaint about government economic encroachment by asking for an official statement regarding the respective roles of public and private enterprise in the national economy (The Straits Times 3/13/77 and 10/1/77).

FOREIGN INVESTMENT AND LOCAL ENTERPRISE

Closely related to the problem of government competition with domestic enterprise is the possibility of direct competition by foreign firms. The literature on the local impact of multinational enterprise often suggests that such firms are in a superior economic position with respect to international market penetration, research and technology, operating efficiency, established brand names, capital, patent protection, and other factors (Turner 1973, chap. 3) and thus may displace and undercut local enterprise (United Nations 1974, chap. 3). This position has been taken as well by such dependency theorists as Frank (1972) and Pena (1975).

There have been cases of direct economic competition with foreign firms. For instance, Lever Brothers has successfully invaded the local consumer market in soap products and ice cream. The Japanese shoe company, Bata, has partially displaced local shoe companies while Japanese shopping centers, such as Yaohan, have successfully lured customers away from local stores. And local construction companies have complained that Japanese firms can outbid local operators because of lower costs resulting from close relationships with other Japanese manufacturers and banks (Asian Wall Street Journal 9/6/77). Particularly distressing has been the tendency for the government to employ Japanese over local firms in housing and other public construction (Far Eastern Economic Review 10/28/77, p. 37). In response to such complaints on the part of local construction firms, the Ministry of National Development responded in 1977 that local companies benefit from the "advanced technological methods" of foreign firms and that this is preferable to "protective measures that may lead to complacency and inefficiency in the construction sector" (Asian Wall Street Journal 9/6/77, p. 10).

By and large, direct product competition between foreign and domestic firms is minimized by the tendency for foreign firms to produce for international, rather than local, markets, unlike the predominantly domestic market oriented local firms. It must be recognized, however, that foreign firms may preempt export market opportunities and in this sense hurt local enterprise.

More important has been the competition for labor and capital inputs. Foreign firms are often in a superior position to attract highly qualified managers, technicians, and workers by virtue of their ability to pay higher wages and salaries than local firms. A recent survey found that salaries of university graduates in American multinational firms were 50 percent higher than those of similarly qualified persons in local firms (The Straits Times 9/2/77).

In most cases, local firms are unable to maintain wage equality
with international firms. In addition, foreign firms are often in an
advantageous position from the standpoint even of local capital mobilization. Since their credit rating is well established, they have
had easier access and at lower interest rates, to both public and
private loans. In recent years, local investment in foreign and joint
venture firms has come to exceed even foreign investment itself
(The Straits Times 3/27/77). Especially important in this regard
is the substantial government equity participation in joint ventures
with foreign capital, particularly in shipbuilding and oil refining.

ENCLAVE INDUSTRIALIZATION AND
LOCAL ENTERPRISE

If some dependency theorists argue that foreign capital dependency "underdevelops" local enterprise because of its superior economic and political position (Frank 1972), others simply maintain
that foreign capital has little positive impact on local enterprise by
virtue of its tendency to be confined to export oriented economic enclaves (Furtado 1970). In particular, it has been argued that recently established, labor-intensive, world market oriented manufacturing in third world countries creates few economic linkages with local
firms. Thus, while such investment may generate wages and employment, it is associated with little structural change or development in local economies (Turner 1973, chap. 7; United Nations 1974,
chap. 3; International Labor Organization 1973, chap. 3). Given
that backward economic linkages and technology transfer are the
most important mechanisms through which foreign enterprise may
stimulate domestic private entrepreneurship, how effectively have
such mechanisms operated in the Singapore context? This question
will be applied to the petroleum and electronics industries, economic
pacesetters during the pre- and post-1968 periods, respectively.
From the standpoint of economic linkages with domestic firms, the
large international petroleum companies in Singapore are integrated
into worldwide marketing and financial systems and import their
major raw material (crude oil) and most of their equipment, while
exporting nearly all their output to other countries within the Pacific
basin. The only significant local stimulus is provided by purchase
of a few locally available items such as tanks, cement, motors,
pipes, and so on, along with local services required for the maintenance and provisioning of oil transport vessels and by the fran-
chise local retailing of oil products.

Technology transfer, the second type of local economic stimulus, refers to the upgrading of skills and knowledge among local

persons in managerial or technical positions, as well as the development of localized research and development capacity.

In addressing the problem of the upgrading and advancement of local personnel into high-level positions in international firms, one must distinguish between internationalization and localization policies. The first of these is found among very large and genuinely international firms such as petroleum companies and large American banks operating in many different countries. In such firms, management in a given country often comprises a variety of nationalities and is not necessarily dominated by persons from either host or home country. In Singapore such a policy often actually discourages locals from aspiring to high-level positions since career mobility may require posting in other countries. On the other hand, their extensive needs for technical skills have encouraged petroleum companies to make substantial investments in the technical training of local workers. Shell Oil, for example, established the first welding school in Singapore and has contributed substantially to the local pool of skilled technicians.

If the older style, more capital-intensive foreign investment did permit some technology transfer to the local economy, what can be said of the economic impact of newer labor-intensive industries such as electronics?

In a recent study of a large sample of electronics firms (Pang and Lim 1977), it was found that the percentage of local to total material production inputs was quite low in most firms, especially in the economically dominant U.S. firms, which obtained an average of only 10 percent of their production inputs locally. The corresponding figure for Japanese firms was 20 percent. Only in the few European firms in the industry did local inputs reach 40 percent to 50 percent, mainly because of the desire among these firms to qualify for GSP tariff reductions on their exports to EEC countries. In part because of quality and price considerations, local inputs are confined to a number of locally available metal parts, plastic cases, and printing and other services (Asian Wall Street Journal 12/14/77). A secondary constraint in local sourcing for U.S. firms is the fact that import tariffs in the United States, to which most of their output is shipped, varies inversely with the percentage of inputs from the United States (Pang and Lim 1977, p. 12).

Unlike the management internationalization policies of large oil companies, true localization policies tend more often to be officially espoused in electronics and precision engineering firms in Singapore. Since the government has not pressed foreign firms to replace expatriate with local managers, localization efforts are based primarily on a desire to reduce salary and benefit costs at management levels (Business Times 2/9/78). Despite localization policies, a large proportion of managers in such firms are drawn from parent companies. This is a consequence of the relative newness of these firms to Singapore, the strong professional and technical background required of management, and a possible disinclination to give locals access to advanced technological information in this highly competitive industry. Such firms also require large numbers of middle-level foreign technicians during startup periods and whenever technical or product changes are being introduced. In the context of rapid technological evolution, this means a frequent and continuing need for foreign technicians. For nontechnical management positions, such firms do tend to localize positions which require substantial local contacts, with the result that local managers are generally found in marketing, personnel, and public relations. (Conversely, in the banks, expatriate managers are often preferred for key local contact positions because many such contacts are in fact with other foreign firms.) Generally, the Japanese firms, because of a lesser cost differential between hiring local and foreign managers, language barriers, more recent establishment, and closer contact with home offices in Japan, are even less advanced than the U.S. and European firms in management localization (Ahmad 1975).

Electronics firms employ mainly low-skilled workers and thus do not have extensive in-house training programs. Similarly, most of these firms engage in little local product development or basic research. Only for locally marketed consumer goods is there effort to adapt world standardized products to the local market. Such adaption is quite limited and confined mainly to modifying design specifications from overseas.

The major exception to a general lack of technology transfer in labor-intensive foreign industry is the somewhat greater tendency particularly among European firms to become involved in joint industry government training programs. Philips and Rollei, for example, are involved in joint training schemes with government, although there is some Japanese involvement in such programs as well (Tan 1979). These firms, it may be noted, tend to produce finished consumer products for regional as well as world markets and have attained a greater degree of vertical integration of their production facilities in Singapore. Thus, their commitment to local training, development, and public relations is somewhat greater than that of the more numerous "foot-loose" U.S. and Japanese companies.

Finally, it must be pointed out that the local supply needs of foreign firms have as often stimulated production in other foreign firms as in domestic ones. Hitachi's Singapore plant, for example, is an important supplier of printed circuits for other foreign electronic companies. And while the major European and U.S. banks do substantial business with domestic firms, much of their activity centers around the needs of regional and Singapore-based international firms. The more recently established small European and Japanese banks are far less involved in domestic business and mainly serve the needs of other same-nationality firms. Similarly, international firms use mainly foreign companies for their auditing needs.

For these reasons, the newer wave of labor-intensive foreign investment, although generating substantial new employment, may provide very little economic impetus to local enterprise.

NEW GOVERNMENT EFFORTS TO ENCOURAGE LOCAL ENTREPRENEURSHIP

It was originally assumed that the managerial and technical training local employees received in foreign firms would ultimately boost local industry when these employees began to establish their own companies (Pang and Tan 1972, p. 129). This assumption has not been borne out, in part because the training these employees have received lends itself less to entrepreneurship than to bureaucratic mobility (see Hoselitz 1960, pp. 144-49), and partly because locals in foreign firms typically lack access to the requisite capital.

Government leaders have become increasingly cognizant of lack of indigenous entrepreneurship. In 1977, Goh Chok Tong, Minister of State (Finance), stressed that "if we are going to make it on our own steam, . . . we should have our own expanding pool of local entrepreneurs. . . . We must identify the reasons for the slow emergence of local industrialists. . . ." And the following year, the Finance Minister, Hon Sui Sen, noted that "We have yet to see any substantial development of local entrepreneurial ability in the manufacturing sector" (both quoted in Tan 1979).

In recognition of the continuing problem of economic stagnation in the private domestic sector and a declining trend in local investment since 1973 (see Table 4.6) (Far Eastern Economic Review 6/3/77), the government has made recent efforts to promote local industry and services. In response to an appeal by the Singapore Manufacturers' Association, a predominantly local body, the government has relaxed its requirements of advance payment of rental and public service charges by firms moving into publicly owned flatted factories in industrial estates (The Straits Times 4/21/77). The Economic Development Board has also expanded its local industries section to advise and assist local business in matters of expansion, training, and diversification. Other efforts to directly assist local business include a Small Industries Finance Scheme, an

TABLE 4.6

Foreign and Local Investment Commitments
in Manufacturing, 1973–77

Year	Total Investment (million Singapore dollars)	Local Investment (million Singapore dollars)	Foreign Investment (million Singapore dollars)	Local Investment as a Percent of Total
1973	944.1	260.6	683.5	27.6
1974	821.8	140.2	681.6	17.1
1975	400.4	133.1	267.3	33.2
1976	364.2	69.5	294.7	19.1
1977	431.0	40.5	390.5	9.4

Source: Singapore International Chamber of Commerce, Investor's Guide, July 1978, p. 68.

Export Credit Insurance Scheme, a Capital Assistance Scheme, a Ship Financing Scheme, a Product Development Assistance Scheme, and increased support for EDB's Joint Venture Bureau (The Straits Times 3/25/77). Legislative requirements for pioneer status have been relaxed somewhat to permit firms with assets of less than $1 million to qualify (The Straits Times 8/20/75), and greater effort is being made to enhance local technological development through the National Productivity Board and the Applied Research Corporation. Several qualifying remarks must be made, however, concerning these new government initiatives. First, they mainly emphasize the development of local supply industries for foreign firms (The Straits Times 6/23/78) and thus may ultimately succeed only in replacing economic dualism with greater dependency on foreign capital. Related to this is the continuing encouragement of joint ventures as a way of stimulating technology transfer. Such a strategy, unaccompanied by government incentives or sanctions, is unlikely to prove successful in the private sector. The trend toward increasingly centralized decision making in large international U.S. corporations (United Nations 1974, chap. 2) makes it unlikely that they will readily enter into joint ventures except perhaps with government. Japanese firms have often established such ventures in the past, in part because of pressure from their home government. However, even they are now buying up local equity shares and becoming increasingly reluctant to enter into partnerships with local capital.

Third, the new efforts to encourage domestic industrial entrepreneurship often clash with other government measures which reduce their significance. For instance, increased encouragement of local industry is countered by a continuing stress on export capacity and higher technology, two criteria which place local firms at a disadvantage in their attempts to obtain government assistance. And government encouragement of greater vertical integration of industrial firms in order to increase local value-added in exports may stimulate further diversification within the foreign sector rather than expansion of domestic support industries. Rollei, for example, has been able to establish its own local capacity to build the tools, equipment, and parts needed for camera manufacture, rather than seeking to purchase these from local suppliers.

CONCLUSION

In this chapter it has been seen that the institutional, legislative, and other measures adopted to induce rapid development through export oriented manufacturing have resulted in massive foreign investment in labor-intensive industry. Such investment has been associated with a relative stagnation in local private enterprise, only in part because of product-market competition. The more important reasons for domestic economic stagnation in the dynamic manufacturing sector relate to factor market competition and, more importantly, to government policy that, in fact if not in intent, has favored international over domestic private investors. Contrary to some suggestions that a positive government orientation toward the needs of foreign capital is based on the power of multinational enterprise to affect public policy (International Labor Organization 1973, chap. 4), the Singapore experience suggests that government industrialization policy has been based primarily on economic considerations. The relative autonomy of public policy making vis-a-vis potential pressures from multinational corporations is based in part on competition among the increasingly numerous foreign firms themselves and in part on the diversity of nationalities of Singapore based foreign firms (see Table 4.4) (Kassalow 1978).

In the next chapter we will discuss the social impact of Singapore's dualistic industrialization experience for local community structures and for the emerging industrial labor force. It will be argued that this multifaceted impact has further reinforced the existing pattern of authoritarian corporatism in industrial relations.

5
WORLD MARKET ORIENTED INDUSTRIALIZATION AND AUTHORITARIAN CORPORATISM

It has been seen that Singapore's recent industrial transforma- ⌡
tion has been based largely on foreign investment in labor-intensive,
export oriented manufacturing. In this chapter we ask how some
economic characteristics of this development pattern have affected
the system established earlier of authoritarian corporatist industrial relations. It will be suggested that (1) employment growth and
the creation of a modern welfare state, both based on rapid industrialization, have legitimated authoritarian rule within a largely
paternalistic framework; (2) economic structural simplification has
supported labor's consolidation into a few large unions linked closely to the NTUC and PAP; (3) economic dualism and a preempting of
new economic opportunities by foreign firms and the state have been
associated with a demobilization and growing dependency of local
business classes and community structures and thus have neutralized
sources of potential, organized opposition to PAP rule; (4) disproportionate growth in the secondary employment sector has been associated with continuing social atomism in the industrial work force.
Such atomism, in turn, has had two opposed consequences for corporatist controls, since it has simultaneously reduced the likelihood
of labor opposition to authoritarian corporatism and also undercut
the social anchorage for effective corporatist institutions, especially
unions.

EMPLOYMENT, WELFARE, AND POLITICAL LEGITIMATION

Because of capital-intensive industry, wage controls, the
creation of employment for a very few relatively well-paid workers,
regional inequalities, and the channeling of benefits to a very small

percentage of the total population, dependent development is often associated with growing economic inequality (Furtado 1970; Chase-Dunn 1975; Apter 1976).

In fact, there is some evidence of this effect in Singapore. First, wage controls have been applied mainly to lower-skilled workers, and not to persons at higher-skill levels (Chen 1972, p. 10), with the result that the income gap between unskilled and skilled workers in Singapore is one of the largest in the entire Asia-Pacific region (Josey 1976, p. 16). Income data for the total population, however, suggest that overall inequality has not increased (Pang 1975), in part because of the magnitude of employment generation, and in part because such employment provides income opportunities to substantial numbers of young females who can thus contribute to family earnings among lower-income families. In addition, rapid economic growth has generated almost full employment as well as a politically neutral (because largely foreign) economic resource base for the provision of social services and infrastructure unparalleled in other countries of the region.

The importance of such economic factors for political legitimacy is clear. The People's Action Party, campaigning consistently and exclusively on its economic record, has captured all parliamentary seats during recent elections and has begun even to entertain the possibility of creating special parliamentary seats for university professors in order to generate more adequate legislative debate.

It is true, of course, that economic growth typically generates political support for any kind of political regime, corporatist or other. But the Singapore experience presents two further considerations. First, it is unlikely that effective authoritarian controls could have been maintained without the policy choice of world market oriented, foreign-based industrialization that has permitted extremely rapid, if dependent, economic growth. Alternate, and probably slower, development strategies would likely have necessitated increasing reliance on police and military coercion in the absence of popular support. Second, Singapore's corporatist wage controls have been accompanied by a tendency for industrial earnings to be redistributed to workers less through direct wage payments than via state welfare expenditures. This has enhanced both legitimacy and dependency-based control in the context of growing state paternalism.

DUALISTIC DEVELOPMENT AND TRADE UNION CONSOLIDATION

Ingham (1974), in his comparative study of British and Scandinavian industrial relations, argues that the relatively greater degree

of union centralization in Sweden and Norway are in part a product
of their simpler industrial structure, centered on a few, highly concentrated export industries. As seen in Chapter 4, such industrial
concentration has characterized Singapore's industrialization, as
well, and has encouraged organization of labor into a few very large
national unions. Such a pattern is seen most clearly in the cases of
the Singapore Industrial Labour Organization (SILO) and the Pioneer
Industries Employees' Union (PIEU), two large industrial unions
which by 1975 represented a very large proportion of workers in
manufacturing and nearly 40 percent of all unionized workers (The
Straits Times 8/3/75). Table 5.1 shows the growing average size
of Singapore's trade unions after 1970. In this way, industrial development has supported the consolidation of a highly centralized
trade union structure closely linked to the PAP.

TABLE 5.1

Number of Trade Unions and Their Membership*

Period	Number of Unions	Percentage of Workforce Organized	Total Union Membership	Average Size of Unions
1960	130	—	144,770	1,114
1961	124	—	164,462	1,326
1962	122	—	189,032	1,549
1963	112	—	142,936	1,276
1964	106	—	157,050	1,482
1965	108	—	154,052	1,426
1966	108	25.9	141,925	1,314
1967	106	—	130,053	1,227
1968	110	—	125,518	1,141
1969	110	—	120,053	1,091
1970	102	17.3	112,488	1,103
1971	100	—	124,350	1,244
1972	97	—	166,988	1,722
1973	92	—	191,481	2,081
1974	90	24.7	203,561	2,262
1975	89	25.0	208,561	2,343
1976	91	25.5	221,936	2,439

*Annual total at end of period.
Source: Ministry of Labour.

INDUSTRIALIZATION, THE BOURGEOISIE,
AND LOCAL COMMUNITIES

The discussion in Chapter 4 suggests a fundamental change in the nature of the indigenous business class. While income and standard of living may be little affected, the independent businessman is more and more replaced by the bureaucrat in the large state or foreign firm on one hand and the investor-rentier on the other. And, even where local enterprise remains viable, it typically becomes increasingly dependent not so much on other local firms as on large outside organizations. Operating beyond the bounds of the local community, this new dependent elite is thus freed from the need to maintain good economic standing within the local community through contributions of money and time to community institutions and associations. Instead, economic resources are increasingly diverted to private consumption, investment, and financial speculation.

A second and related consequence of dualistic development is that a shift in economic opportunity from local to modern-sector firms draws especially young persons away from the communal sector into outside employment. For example, a striking characteristic of Singapore's industrialization is the rapid mobilization of young, single females who, in earlier periods, would more likely have remained at home in unpaid family employment or worked in a family business.

A consequence of the movement of young persons into outside employment is a decline in the economic basis for kinship bonds and loss of control by elders (but see Tilly and Scott 1978, p. 228). This is largely the result of the new freedom of young persons who are no longer economically dependent on their elders. Lim (1974), in the study of young female workers in a Jurong textile factory, found that many of the women worked in part to establish their independence of family control, and they fulfilled their family obligations largely by giving part of their earnings to parents (also see Chua 1973). Such enhanced independence of females applies as well for the increasing numbers of married women who are taking up outside employment (Tan 1976).

Accompanying the shift in employment opportunities is an increasing stress on English-medium, technical or vocational education (Kuo 1978). In part, this is a consequence of government policy, beginning with the creation, in 1968, of a Technical Education Department and the expenditure the following year of $17 million to institute high school level technical education (Asian Business & Industry 1972). In part too, however, it is the result of parental recognition of the greater economic value of English-medium education. By the mid-1970s, even college graduates of the Chinese-medium Nanyang University were having trouble finding jobs (Far Eastern Economic Review 11/19/76). English enrollments increased from 50.4 percent of the total in 1962 to 64.8 percent in 1972 (Doraisamy 1969; Ministry of Education 1972) and have continued to grow since then. This has resulted in reduced exposure on the part of young people to the traditional classics and morality (Gamer 1971).

A third important factor in isolating young workers from family and community control is that of protracted physical separation. Many young men and women working in Jurong factories, for instance, live in dormitories or residential flats provided by employers. Similarly, young working couples often move into government flats provided for workers in or near industrial estates. This, along with frequent reliance on shift work in factories, effectively isolates workers from community social life (K. Y. Chang 1973).

All these factors associated with Singapore's recent dualistic industrialization, along with those government housing, education, and political policies that were themselves part of a broader strategy of world market oriented industrialization and political consolidation, have led to an attenuation of dialect community identities and bonds (Hassan 1976, p. 260), as shown by growing outmarriage rates (Lim 1974; Tan 1976; Ibrahim 1977) and by an increasing loss both of elder control over children and of mother-tongue fluency (Chiang 1977).

Geiger has described the importance of economic independence in loosening familial bonds, an important basis for larger communal loyalties among Chinese:

> Occupational roles increasingly involved activity outside the household or economic relationships with strangers. . . . So, too, did education and vocational training in governmentally or privately supported schools, medical care, recreational activities, and an expanding range of other satisfactions formerly obtained within the family. . . . The status of the women members of the family steadily improved especially as employment opportunities for unmarried girls gradually arose in the service trades and later in manufacturing industry. . . . These changes inevitably reduced the extent of the individual's identification with the family and fostered a sense of self-identity . . . loyalties to the nonfamily institutions—employing organizations, trade unions, eventually political parties, etc.—which served individual interests in various ways began to reduce the previously overriding commitment to the family interest per se. Self-determining interpersonal

> relations became increasingly important, especially
> among young people who insisted upon having more
> and more of a voice in the choice of friends, spouses,
> vocations, and recreation . . . (Geiger 1973, p. 58).

While Geiger's description relates primarily to the family, it applies with equal force to community loyalties and identification.

The critical importance of economic factors in ethnic community decline is shown by the continued vitality of dialect communities which <u>have</u> retained viable economic bases during the recent period of growth. In the Cantonese community, for instance, traditional artisan skills and subcontracting systems have provided a strong basis for recruitment, apprenticeship, and labor control in the modern shipbuilding and repair industry where contract labor systems are still widely used (<u>The Straits Times</u> 2/8/75). Depending on the yard, approximately 20 percent to 60 percent of shipyard labor is recruited through subcontracting in order to retain workload flexibility and also because workers thus recruited do not fall under the purview of most labor legislation. Similarly, the Hengua dialect community retains its cohesion through continuing control over vehicle parts distribution and control of much of the tire and retread business. Hengua-controlled firms in fact act as distributors for such companies as Ford, Cycle and Carriage (makers of Mercedes-Benz), Firestone, and Michelin. The only major recent threat to the economic position of the Hengua group is increasing reliance by public bus and taxi fleets on their own internal distribution and repair systems (<u>The Straits Times</u> 1/25/77).

Through its tendency both to undercut the vitality and economic independence of domestic business classes and to disrupt local community structures, dualistic industrialization has tended to eliminate the leadership and organizational bases for the mobilization of an effective external challenge to authoritarian political rule. Indicative of the loss of leadership resources for independent interest groups was the great difficulty on the part of the Chinese Chamber of Commerce in locating a prominent businessman willing to take on the responsibilities and expenses of chamber presidency in 1977.

INTERNAL CONSEQUENCES: SOCIAL ATOMISM IN THE EMERGING INDUSTRIAL WORKFORCE

Dualistic industrialization in Singapore has been associated with a disproportionate growth in low-wage, semiskilled jobs in labor absorbing foreign films and with an expansion of employment in what Piore describes as the "secondary" sector, in which "jobs tend to be low-paying, with poorer working conditions [than in the primary sector], little chance of advancement, . . . considerable instability in jobs and a high turnover among the labor force" (Piore, quoted in Montagna 1977, p. 68).

Workers in Singapore's foreign, export-oriented firms experience continuing job insecurity. Offshore production is highly responsive to fluctuations in international markets and is generally able to quickly reduce local production without incurring substantial economic losses. An indication of the generally greater responsiveness of foreign than of local firms to international economic conditions is a relatively greater decline in foreign investment levels during the recession of 1974-75 (see Table 4.6). But more important is the fact that a large percentage of layoffs during that period was among workers in large, foreign, export-oriented firms. Of the 16,900 workers retrenched during 1974, 66 percent were in electronics alone (Tan 1976), and in this industry, 67 percent of the U.S. firms, versus only 30 percent of the Singapore firms, resorted to retrenchment (Pang and Lim 1977).

A second characteristic of much of the new industrial employment is the lack of opportunity for career mobility among production workers, as reflected in the fact that supervisors in Western firms, more than in local firms, tend to be externally recruited (Deyo 1978). In part, this is a consequence of an industrial technology that makes it possible to break down complex tasks into simple and easily learned tasks and that underlies the relocation of industry to low-wage countries in the first place. Such a technology is associated with educational and hierarchical gaps between low-skilled workers and supervisory and technical workers. It is also associated with greater stress on educational qualifications for middle-level entry into the firm (Low 1973) and less opportunity for workers to learn new higher-level skills through on-the-job training which might enhance their mobility prospects.

Third, foreign firms rely to a greater extent than do local Chinese firms on formal institutional controls and work inducements, rather than on personal managerial authority. Western firms place far greater stress on formal specification of employee job expectations through written job descriptions and rules. Unlike the intensely personal, if autocratic, authority exercised in the Chinese firm, relations between managers and workers in foreign firms is mediated by rules, unions, and formal contracts (Cheng 1968). That such formalism and impersonality extend to relations with lower-level management as well is suggested by the finding of minimal interaction between workers and supervisors in the electronics industry (Lim Guek Poh 1974).

Fourth, workers in electronics, textiles, and other similar labor-absorbing industries, have jobs which are highly repetitive and monotonous, give minimal autonomy, and involve technologies which often reduce interaction between workers through line assembly operations (electronics) and high noise levels (textiles).

Finally, as suggested earlier, employment in such industries is associated with the social isolation of workers from the larger social context of family, friends, and community.

A second set of characteristics of modern sector industrial employment, particularly after 1968, relates to attributes of the rapidly expanding labor force. As is typical of secondary employment sectors everywhere, the workers in Singapore's new labor-absorbing industries are disproportionately drawn from the ranks of youth, females, immigrants, and others from a variety of ethnic backgrounds, who are handicapped in finding good employment and are therefore willing to accept low wages and undesirable working conditions.

Table 5.2 shows the labor force distribution by industry for the total working population and for females separately during 1966, 1970, and 1974. First may be noted the structural shift in Singapore's economy between 1966 and 1974, during which the percentage of workers in manufacturing, finance, insurance, and transport and communication grew relative to that in other sectors. The greatest increase was in manufacturing, where employment grew by 129,790 workers, thus accounting for 47 percent of the total employment increase during the period. Growth was especially rapid during the 1970-74 period because of the time lag between earlier investment commitments and the beginning of actual operations. Total employment grew by 173,457 during this period, a 26.6 percent gain, with manufacturing accounting for 52.5 percent of total growth.

Much of this growth was in foreign-based firms which located in Singapore and other low-income countries specifically in order to utilize the large numbers of low-skilled workers who could be employed at low wages. Particularly impressive was the tremendous growth in female employment (Wong 1976), which rose by 70.7 percent from 1970 to 1974, versus only 15.1 percent for males, so that female employment expansion accounted for 62.6 percent of the total workforce increase despite substantially lower labor force participation rates. In manufacturing, female employment increased by 118 percent, versus 36 percent for males, thus raising the female share of the manufacturing workforce from 31.3 percent in 1970 to 40 percent in 1974.

Most of the female entrants to the manufacturing sector entered the ranks of semiskilled production workers. It may be noted in Table 5.3 that female employment in this category grew by 48,507,

TABLE 5.2

Working Persons by Industry, 1966, 1970, and 1974[a]

Industry	Total						Female					
	1966[b]		1970		1974		1966[b]		1970		1974	
	Total Number Employed	Percent of Total Employed	Total Number Employed	Percent of Total Employed	Total Number Employed	Percent of Total Employed	Number Employed	Female as Percent of Total Females	Number Employed	Female as Percent of Total Females	Number Employed	Female as Percent of Total Females
Total	548,030	100.0	650,892	100.0	824,349	100.0	118,230	100.0	153,612	100.0	262,156	100.0
Agriculture, forestry, hunting, and fishing	19,224	3.5	22,458	3.5	21,709	2.6	4,639	3.9	4,796	3.1	6,314	2.4
Mining and quarrying	1,404	0.3	2,168	0.3	1,748	0.2	75	0.1	203	0.1	291	0.1
Manufacturing	104,441	19.0	143,100	22.0	234,231	28.5	23,648	20.0	48,121	31.3	104,950	40.0
Building and construction	34,599	6.3	43,126	6.6	42,495	5.2	2,682	2.3	2,817	1.8	3,982	1.5
Electricity, gas, and water	7,516	1.4	7,615	1.2	10,344	1.3	363	0.3	533	0.3	1,117	0.4
Commerce	155,137[c]	28.3[c]	152,910	23.5	172,650	20.9	25,632[c]	21.7[c]	28,986	18.9	50,168	19.1
Finance, insurance; estates and business services	19,310[d]	3.5[d]	23,071	3.5	46,574	5.6	2,931[d]	2.5[d]	5,305	3.5	15,978	6.1
Transport and communication	54,054	9.9	79,041	12.1	97,519	11.8	2,626	2.2	3,943	2.6	11,170	4.3
Services	148,550	27.1	177,022	27.2	195,136	23.7	55,245	46.7	58,843	38.2	67,506	25.8
Others	3,795	0.7	381	0.1	1,943	0.2	389	0.3	63	0.04	680	0.3

aEconomically active persons who have not worked previously are not included.

b1966 figures have been adjusted to make the categories comparable with those of 1970 and 1974.

cRestaurants and hotels have been excluded from "Services" and included in "Commerce" as in 1970 and 1974.

dFinancial institutions, insurance, real estate, and business services have been taken out of "Commerce" and "Service" categories and placed in the category "Finance, insurance, real estate and business services" as in 1970 and 1974.

Sources: Singapore Sample Household Survey 1966, Report on the Census of Population of Singapore 1970, and 1974 Labour Force Report.

TABLE 5.3

Absolute and Percentage Change in Female Employment
in Selected Occupations and Industries, 1970–74

Females	Industry					
	Manufacturing	Commerce	Transport and Communication	Finance	Service	Others
Professional and technical						
Absolute change	+1,220	+357	+371	+1,397	+4,275	+381
Percentage change	+283	+158	+562	+461	+21	+680
Clerical						
Absolute change	+5,199	+9,314	+5,691	+7,790	+4,058	+1,034
Percentage change	+126	+144	+218	+173	+56	+98
Sales						
Absolute change	+761	+8,352	+69	+266	+468	+41
Percentage change	+152	+54	+246	+216	+287	+513
Service						
Absolute change	+880	+2,904	+512	+796	-2,839	+182
Percentage change	+114	+56	+141	+627	-9.8	+294
Production						
Absolute change	+48,507	+102	+604	+438	+629	+267
Percentage change	+115	+8	+75	+456	+86	+11
Others						
Absolute change	+266	+159	-20	-13	+2,451	+1,567
Percentage change	+121	+89	-29	-8	+1,114	+33

Sources: 1970 Census, p. 169; 1974 Labour Force Report, pp. 84–86.

accounting for nearly half of total female employment growth. By 1974, over half of all manufacturing production workers were female (Deyo and Chen 1976). Many of the females who entered manufacturing during this period went into such new labor-absorbing industries as electronics and textiles, with electronics alone accounting for 56 percent of the total female employment growth in manufacturing.

A large number of the new female workers are young and single. In 1974, 25.6 percent were below the age of 19, and 70.9 percent were below 29. This involved an increase in the number of younger female workers from 1966, when 21.9 percent of the female labor force was below the age of 19 and 55.7 below 29. (Similarly, the percentage of male workers below the age of 29 increased moderately, from 29.8 percent in 1966 to 46.6 percent in 1974. The major increases in female labor force participation rates during 1966-70 were among young single females, while those for 1970-74 occurred among young married females, in part because of tightening job market and in part because of increasing provision of childcare facilities in public housing estates.)

If a large proportion of the new industrial workforce was young, female, and single, another of its characteristics was an increasing percentage of immigrant workers attracted to expanding job opportunities in Singapore. By 1973, over 100,000 of Singapore's approximately 800,000 workers were reported to be immigrant workers (Pang and Kay 1974), admitted to take on some of the jobs for which labor shortages had begun to appear.

A final characteristic of the growing labor force was its ethno-cultural heterogeneity within employing organizations. Whereas firms in the communal sector had employed persons of substantial similarity in dialect and ethnic background, the new industries largely disregarded such factors. In a survey of industrial establishments taken in 1975, supervisors in large Western firms reported the use of three to five languages or dialects in their work units, with heavy reliance on pidginized versions of Malay and Hokkien. A second survey of shipyards in Singapore showed that among ten small local yards the single largest ethnic or dialect group in each yard comprised an average of 75 percent of the total workforce, as against 41 percent in the generally larger government, joint-venture, and foreign yards (Heyzer 1971). Such heterogeneity among workers is accentuated in many firms by the presence of foreign management at higher organizational levels.

WORLD MARKET ORIENTED INDUSTRIALIZATION AND WORKFORCE ATOMISM

These characteristics of modern industrial employment in Singapore have been associated with a continuing attenuation of social bonds in industrial life, undercutting attachments of workers both to firm and coworkers. In part, this is a consequence of lack of upward job mobility and insecurity of employment, with a resulting weak organizational commitment (Moore 1965, chap. 5) and low social involvement in the job. In addition, employers in such cheap labor industries as electronics and textiles, where worker training often takes less than a month, may decide not to attempt to stabilize their workforces through changes in wage scales or working conditions, since they may often actually benefit from high rates of turnover that keep the total wage bill down by reducing seniority wage increments among workers. Reliance on impersonal rules, contractual agreements, union intermediaries, and benchflow or machine workpacing reduces the potential development of personal relationships with superiors. Interacting mainly with machines or instruments rather than with other workers has the further effect of isolating workers from one another. In a textile plant surveyed in 1976, each woman worked alone on a row of spindles under her responsibility. In most cases, she worked back to back with another woman and was within five meters or so of a third worker in the next row; but high noise levels effectively reduced conversation that, in any case, would have been in violation of company rules (Deyo 1980).

The economic dualism which characterizes the relationship between the new industrial sector and the domestic economy is accompanied by social dualism. It was noted earlier that modern industrial employment results in the social isolation of workers from family and community. Such isolation is associated with another facet of social dualism, lack of carryover of existing social commitments into industrial employment. Unlike local firms whose organizational stability and authority are in part stabilized by social commitments to job sponsors, family, and local associations, employment relations in modern industry are based almost exclusively on financial considerations, thus lending a quality of fragility and expediency to such relations. Such an institutional bypassing of traditional social bonds applies not only to organizational commitments but to union involvement as well, since modern unions have essentially been imposed from the top down, rather than evolving from earlier-existing guild or craft workers' associations. Such a pattern of social dualism stands in marked contrast to the historical experience of European countries in which craft and occupational loyalties along with traditional forms of economic authority provided a basis for the long-term development of new industrial commitments.

The fact that dualistic development in Singapore has been based on the attraction of low wage groups of youth, females, and immigrants into low-skill industrial employment has had further consequences for associational bonds in industry. First, young single females, numerically the most important group of new industrial workers, often stop working when they marry or have their first child (Chua 1973). Similarly, young workers, whether male or female, often look at their first job as a temporary source of income and experience before moving on to better employment, preferably in white-collar positions (Pang and Lim 1977). Immigrant workers, of course, are often target workers and expect to return home after saving or earning a certain amount of money. And married female workers, while far more stable than singles, often experience career interruptions due to family circumstances such as the birth of a child.

Thus, the various characteristics of the work situation and labor force associated with the expanding secondary employment sector have perpetuated fragile and atomistic social attachments to firms and coworkers in Singapore's modern industrial sector. Most easily documented is the very weak organizational commitment of workers. A 1969 report on labor force problems in new factories indicated quit rates of 10 percent to 20 percent per month, or 120 percent to 240 percent per annum in some factories. At that time, Texas Instruments, a United States-based electronics firm, reported quit rates at 6.5 percent to 15 percent per month, versus around 2 percent in its U.S. plants (The Straits Times 11/24/69). In 1976 the Economic Development Board reported that overall voluntary resignations in manufacturing had averaged 4.4 percent per month or 52.8 percent in 1975 (Ngiam 1977), approximately double the U.S. rate in manufacturing (U.S. Dept. of H.E.W. 1973), and down somewhat from 5.4 percent in 1973. In general, rates are highest among low-skilled workers in the rapidly growing, mass production, export oriented firms which have flourished during the rapid industrial development of the past decade. In 1973 the Ministry of Labor reported annual turnover rates of nearly 95 percent in electronics and 100 percent in a textile plant that had been visited by officials.

Related to such high turnover rates are very high rates of absenteeism. A 1976 report indicated absenteeism in Singapore was higher than that in other countries in the region (The Straits Times 6/28/76). Again, as in the case of turnover, the highest rates are to be found in electronics. The general manager of an electronics firm indicated, in a personal communication, that he faced absenteeism rates of over 10 percent per month.

Industrial employment is similarly characterized by atomistic relationships among workers themselves. Chang finds a restricted social life, lack of group formation, and low organizational membership among male factory workers in Jurong (Chang 1973). Further evidence of such atomism comes from a recent study of 24 female workers in the spinning section of a Taiwan-based textile factory in Singapore (Deyo 1980). These workers placed greater stress on coworker relations than on any other job factor as a source of potential, job-related gratification. To develop close relations with coworkers was seen as more important than any other aspect of the job, including pay. These relations were seen as potentially providing mutual assistance on the job, group entertainment to reduce job monotony, and mutual support in dealings with superiors, who were seen as distant and unconcerned about their feelings and welfare. Yet, despite the psychological centrality of the workgroup, the workers generally felt that coworkers failed to provide mutual assistance on the job or support in dealings with superiors. In addition, references were made throughout the interviews to problems of gossip, feuding, and interpersonal competition.

There is an important exception to the general pattern of interpersonal atomism among Singapore industrial workers. In part, perhaps because employers often encourage workers to bring friends in to apply for vacancies, workers may maintain close personal relationships with one or two other workers in a given firm. Chua (1973), in her study of electronics workers, found that approximately half her sample were induced to apply for work by a friend who was already employed.

This pattern was discovered as well in the textile study, where it was found that sociometric friendship choices among workers bore little relationship to patterns of physical proximity on the shop floor but displayed a very close relationship to dates of recruitment. The sociometric pattern itself was characterized by isolated dyads and triads consisting mainly of women who had applied for work at approximately the same time. The personnel director in this firm reported that women not only came in with friends but quit together as well. And it was learned, several months after the initial interviews had been completed, that many of those who had by that time quit, left with a close friend. These small friendship cliques, which derived cohesiveness from sources independent of the work situation in particular firms, appeared to move frequently from firm to firm and generally in response to job boredom and small differences in pay (Deyo 1980).

It should be noted that weak coworker attachments may strongly affect attachments to the firm. Several investigators have found that a powerful predictor of organizational turnover in Singapore is the extent of involvement in workgroups and job-based friendships (Heyzer 1974; Lim Guek Poh 1974). And in the textile study discussed earlier, it was found that 67 percent of those workers not chosen as a friend by another worker, versus 27 percent of those who were chosen, had left their jobs three months later.

CORPORATISM AND UNION ATTACHMENTS

If attachments to firm and workgroup are fragile and expediency-based in Singapore's secondary labor market, union attachments, at least until recently, have been equally weak. Union membership, an important indicator of social integration of the labor force, showed serious decline during the late 1960s. As shown in Table 5.3, there have been two periods of union membership decline. The first, in 1963, was the result of union deregistration during the premerger political struggle between the PAP and The Barisan Socialis. But membership again declined from the 154,052 figure for the end of 1965 to 112,488 in 1970, despite very rapid increases in employment during this period. In percentage terms, 26 percent of employed persons were union members in 1966, versus only 17 percent in 1970. Union membership in NTUC affiliates, which have contained over 90 percent of unionized workers during recent years (Gan 1977), dropped from 112,635 in 1965, to 85,422 in 1969.

Similarly, the orientation of many workers toward their unions is marked by short-term expediency. During a conversation with the personnel director of an electronics firm, it was learned that paid-up union membership in the local SILO branch had dropped markedly in 1977, immediately after the announcement of a small increase in membership dues.

In part, weak union attachments may be attributed to high rates of organizational turnover. Anticipation of short organizational tenure likely reduces union participation levels. Similarly, it may be explained by the labor force heterogeneity discussed earlier, which is mirrored in union membership. A study of NTUC-affiliated unions, to which workers in modern industry often belong, revealed far greater ethnic diversity in those unions than in the typically smaller nonaffiliated unions primarily representing workers in small, traditional enterprises (Heyzer and Wee 1972). Such heterogeneity, which would tend to reduce workgroup cohesion, tends to undercut union solidarity as well.

On the other hand, the fact that the decline in union membership began in 1965 suggests that the causes of weak union attachments must be sought in social changes predating the recent industrial transformation, particularly those associated with the imposition of authoritarian corporatism in industrial relations.

First, the very success of institutional intervention by the state, particularly during the mid-1960s, depended upon the destruction of many preexisting, solidary economic groups, especially the communal and leftist trade unions that were associated with the Barisan Socialis. Second, substantive regulation of industrial relations, increasing reliance on government arbitration of industrial conflict, and legislative elimination of several employment issues from collective bargaining have greatly diminished the instrumental significance of unions for workers. Pang (1976) reports, in this regard, a lack of positive relationship between union membership and earnings among industrial workers. Mr. Quek, a prominent NTUC leader, referred to this problem in 1970:

> The present period of declining [union] membership coincides with a period when the rank and file membership looks more to the Ministers for leadership than the trade union movement itself, and has come to regard the NTUC as but another government department to which it owes no loyalty and for which, however impalatable it is to say, it has scant respect (quoted in Heyzer and Wee 1972, p. 7).

Third, was the increasing tendency for union policy decisions to be made at national, rather than local levels, thus reducing rank-and-file involvement in union decision making. The increasing size of unions (see Table 5.1), another consequence of the government policy of centralization and consolidation of the labor movement, has had a similar effect of reducing rank-and-file participation and involvement in union life. Finally, the very success of Singapore's industrial relations system in reducing conflict has likely also reduced that union solidarity which normally results from some degree of intergroup conflict.

WORKFORCE ATOMISM: AN ALTERNATIVE EXPLANATION

A common explanation for the weak organizational and union attachments of such groups as women and youth refers less to situational and structural factors relating to occupational and political life than to their presumably weaker occupational involvement than other groups. Pang, for example, argues that workforce instability among Singapore's female workers is explained in part by the fact that work, for them, is not a central life interest (Pang and Kay 1974). In order to determine whether situational factors such as those relating to family and employment are more or less important than work orientation factors, comparative longitudinal data on the work orientation of various categories of workers would be needed. Lacking such data, we may refer to survey data on blue-collar industrial workers gathered by a class of University of Singapore undergraduate sociology students during 1974.

The most unstable group of industrial workers, from the standpoints of job turnover and union participation, is that of single, young females (Ho 1974). Table 5.4 compares the responses of these workers to those of other groups on a questionnaire item asking how important they felt each of a number of job factors was for their feelings of personal satisfaction. First, it may be noted that the average overall percentage of single female respondents saying these various factors were "very important" is 63 percent, not appreciably lower than that of skilled males and far higher than that of married females. This suggests that work may be as important a central life interest for this group as for other more stable groups. The ranking of job factors in terms of relative importance further suggests that single female workers are no more expedient and pecuniary and are as concerned about intrinsic and social occupational rewards as others. First, they place no greater emphasis on pay and less on raises and benefits than other groups, with the single exception that skilled males are somewhat less concerned about pay. Nor can their relatively higher organizational turnover rates be explained by a lack of desire to establish good social relationships with coworkers and supervisors, since they place greater absolute and relative stress on both factors than do other categories of workers.

While these work orientation findings are subject to a number of alternate interpretations, they do suggest that institutional constraints and other situational factors may be as or more important than a presumed weaker or more expedient work orientation in explaining the high job mobility of this group of workers (also see Ho 1974).

WORKFORCE ATOMISM AND
AUTHORITARIAN CORPORATISM

Recent industrialization has been associated with growing workforce atomism whose economic consequences will be discussed in Chapter 6. But what of its consequences for authoritarian corporatism? Workforce atomism relating to the workplace and coworkers implies a demobilization of labor groups and solidarities which might challenge elite-imposed corporatist structures and a resulting consolidation of authoritarian corporatism. Where there is dissent and protest, as during the 1974-75 recession, it tends to be disorganized and easily contained. Pang notes in this regard that "future labor unrest will probably be of a wildcat nature. Strikes are likely to be small in scale, of limited duration and easily contained because of lack of organization. Industrial peace will not

TABLE 5.4

Percentage of Workers Saying Each Job Factor Was "Very Important"

Job Item	Single Females (N = 88)		Unskilled Married Females (N = 85)		Males (N = 50)		Skilled Males (N = 59)	
	Percent	Rank	Percent	Rank	Percent	Rank	Percent	Rank
Work itself	65	5	40	10	66	6.5	69	6
Work conditions	59	7	31	11	55	8	61	10
Promotions	49	10	42	9	52	9	51	11
Supervision	71	3	51	5.5	50	10	64	8
Coworkers	83	1	54	4	69	4	80	2
Pay	74	2	60	2	82	1.5	76	4
Independence	51	9	43	8	68	5	73	5
Raises	61	6	69	1	82	1.5	66	7
Coworker respect	58	8	46	7	48	11	63	9
Security	70	4	57	3	66	6.5	83	1
Benefits	48	11	51	5.5	78	3	73	3
Average	63		49		65		69	

be threatened . . . and the appearance of . . . harmony will be preserved" (Pang and Kay 1974, p. 27). On the other hand, to the extent such atomism weakens attachments to corporatist structures as well, it undercuts the organizing and disciplining power of corporatism.

These mutually opposed consequences of social atomism reflect the deeper paradox of corporatism: its need for repression and demobilization on one hand and for organization and mobilization on the other. The dilemma is seen even more clearly within the corporatist structure itself. After 1965, the PAP effectively demobilized organized labor along with its potential to challenge the developmental policies of political or economic elites. But such demobilization, reflected in declining union membership, had the unintended effect of undercutting the union structures through which corporatist control was to be exercised.

CONCLUSION

World market oriented industrialization in Singapore has been rapid and successful in its provision of jobs and wages for a growing labor force. And it has provided a politically neutral source of material resources for the building of a paternalistic welfare state. In these ways, it has bolstered the political legitimacy of the ruling party, as reflected in its continued and overwhelming electoral support through the 1970s, during which not one parliamentary seat went to an opposition party.

But the positive consequences for political stability of world market industrialization have taken other more subtle forms as well. It has created an industrial structure which is compatible with centralized, government-controlled union structures. It has undercut the vitality and economic independence of local business classes which in other societies have tended to challenge authoritarian political rule, and it has disrupted local community structures which might have provided the leadership and social support for challenges to corporatist control of unions. Finally, it has led to the emergence of a highly atomistic industrial labor force that lacks the solidarity and commitment to organize against union and government domination.

Chapter 6 discusses some of the negative consequences of workforce atomism for economic growth and for the long-term stability of authoritarian corporatism itself. It concludes with a description of recent government attempts to resolve these problems through industrial community building.

6
CREATING INDUSTRIAL COMMUNITY: TOWARD A CORPORATE PATERNALIST SOCIETY

Increasing social atomism among Singapore's industrial workforce, in part the product of bureaucratic-authoritarian controls and of dualistic industrialization, had tended to undercut the associational basis for commitment to elite-imposed norms, institutions, and policy. This problematic consequence has led to increasing efforts to revitalize associational commitments, especially to union and firm, in order to ensure continued political stability and economic growth. This chapter examines the problematic consequences of workforce atomism for employers, unionists, and political leaders, as well as the approaches such elites have taken to deal with these consequences. It will be shown that the process of adaptation to problems of social atomism has moved Singapore increasingly away from strictly bureaucratic to more popular, paternalistic modes of authoritarian corporatism.

WORKFORCE ATOMISM AND INSTITUTIONAL
DEMORALIZATION: CONSEQUENCES FOR
CONTINUED DEVELOPMENT

Lee Soo Ann, in his discussion of Singapore's economic growth, argues that:

The weakness of the economic system ironically can only be overcome by determined efforts on the part of those placed in and under authority to put the cohesiveness of the country over and above the perennial claims of the economic system itself, to ensure continued growth (Lee Soo Ann 1976, p. 28).

The same point had been stated somewhat differently by Lee Kuan Yew in 1971. In speaking of the negative consequences of English-medium education, the prerequisite for occupational mobility in modern economic life, Lee referred to the "detrimental effects of deculturation" and the creation of "anaemic, up-rooted citizens without the social cohesiveness and cultural impetus that gives the people the drive and will to succeed as a group" (quoted in Josey 1971, p. 346).

In the early period of industrialization, when new firms located in Singapore primarily to utilize low-skilled labor in simple assembly operations, high rates of turnover did not greatly affect productivity or labor costs. This was because job training was short in duration, and new workers could readily be recruited in a labor-surplus economy. During the early 1970s, however, growing labor shortages, as well as need for more extensive inplant training resulting from increasing technological sophistication, began to make high quit rates increasingly costly.

Tenuous organizational loyalties had a number of specific consequences which employers and policy makers found unacceptable. First, of course, were the direct economic costs of low worker morale, apathy, and absenteeism which reduced Singapore's economic competitiveness with such other industrial exporters as Taiwan, South Korea, and Hong Kong. A management consultant has described the problem as follows:

> Singapore's factories desperately need manpower, but up to 25 percent of the national workforce is relatively idle because they are on the hop. . . . The workers expect better pay and all sorts of privileges. They are actually shopping around for them, from factory to factory. . . . This is already making things difficult for foreign investors, forcing them to cut back and subcontract their work. . . . If Singapore loses the investors altogether . . . the national economic growth must necessarily suffer (Sunday Times 6/18/78).

But this consultant's remarks suggest a further and more fundamental problem facing government policy makers as well. Growing labor shortages and increased living costs are exerting upward pressure on industrial wages. Yet, Singapore is competing in its bid to attract foreign investment with neighboring more rural societies with lower living costs and more abundant underemployed labor. The government has attempted several short-run solutions to this problem by admitting immigrant workers and by reducing the age at which children may enter employment. In the longer run, however, the government has tried to encourage technological up-grading and higher labor skills in order to increase labor productiv-ity and thus to keep labor costs competitive (Pang and Tan 1972; Kassalow 1978). Ngiam, EDB chairman, while suggesting that high rates of turnover had contributed to a decline in value-added per worker between 1973 and 1975, also placed the problem in this larger developmental perspective:

> Unlike the earlier industries where skill levels re-quired are not unduly high, better paid jobs we now seek in the relatively more advanced industries de-mand longer, more intensive apprenticeship and train-ing. While such manufacturers, helped by Government, are prepared to train, the cost of such training has to be finally paid for by the individual. He can pay for it by serving his company long and faithfully. Unless there is such a human understanding, or better still moral commitment, Singapore will be condemned to the backwaters of manufacturing (Ngiam 1977).

ELITE RESPONSES

In response to problems of inadequate work discipline, for-eign firms have relied to an even greater degree on formal institu-tional controls. In the study of local and international firms cited earlier (Deyo 1978), it was found that Western firms placed greater emphasis on written job descriptions, as well as on formal job evalu-ations for decisions regarding pay increases for workers.

Similarly, in the case study of the foreign textile factory, it was found that workers were subject to a vast number of rules re-garding on-the-job behavior. These rules specified standards of behavior relating to obedience, respectfulness, cooperation with co-workers, and mode of dress, and even prohibited conversation among workers while on the job. Pay increases, in turn, were partly based on rule compliance.

But such enterprise-level sanctions have been only partially successful. The earlier quoted management consultant who com-plained about the economic costs of high rates of turnover went on to argue that "the firms have done a lot in making employment at-tractive, even compromising on discipline, but to no avail. Only the government is in a position to put out incentives or deterrents to save the [electronics] industry" (Sunday Times 6/18/78).

Government, like employers, has resorted in part to sanc-tions aimed at reducing economically disruptive behavior at the individual level. Particularly important have been explicit provisions built into both law and NWC recommendations to discourage job changing. Immigrant workers, for instance, are not allowed to change employers within three years of arrival without obtaining new work permits (The Straits Times 5/6/73). Under the revised Employment Act of 1975, workers cannot claim retrenchment benefits unless they have worked at least three full years with the same employer. Bonuses have similarly been denied job changers, while the National Wages Council has recommended that yearly wage increases be given only to workers who had been employed more than 12 full months (The Straits Times 6/30/78). Such efforts were extended beyond job turnover problems to tighter controls over work behavior itself. Starting in 1976 and 1977, the NWC has recommended that wage increments be denied those defined as "malingerers": that is, those whose attendance and work quality were unsatisfactory (The Straits Times 1/2/77). This provision, of course, greatly strengthened the power of management to employ merit criteria in employee remuneration.

Such sanctions have been accompanied by intensive public campaigns against "job hopping" and "malingering" among industrial workers by both public officials and union officials. And increased attention was given to problems of company loyalty and commitment in job training programs. In suggesting a new system of apprenticeship training in 1976, for example, the Industrial Training Board defended the system by pointing to one of its major advantages over earlier schemes:

> . . . that the apprentice is committed from the start of training to make the best of a career in that company, at least for a few years, and would be predisposed to develop a loyalty to his colleagues and the organization which would pave the way for a sound and lasting working relationship with the company (The Straits Times 12/1/76).

THE SEARCH FOR SOCIAL-BASED
INSTITUTIONAL COMMITMENTS

It has also been recognized, however, that the longer-term success of policies of increased work productivity, labor stabilization, and wage restraint would depend on the cultivation of deeper moral commitments, as suggested by Ngiam, and that such commitments must, in turn, be rooted in associational loyalties to firm, union, and to the larger community which would ultimately benefit from the efforts and sacrifices demanded of labor for national economic growth.

The industrialization experiences of European and Japanese societies suggest an emergence of industrial order based in part on the carryover and transformation of existing patterns of social organization and in part on the institutionalization of conflict among a number of social groups created or affected by economic change. In these cases, the state played a relatively minor, and largely reactive, role in establishing industrial order. Quite different is the industrialization experience of Singapore. First, rapid dualistic development has bypassed those established forms of social organization that might have provided a basis for a new institutional order, and second, corporatist controls have eliminated autonomous labor organizations that have participated in institution building under more liberal political regimes. For these reasons, Singapore's political and, to a far lesser degree, economic elites have had to play a crucial role in unilaterally creating a basis for new associational bonds in industrial life. If group and organizational bonds were to grow in the socially inhospitable environment of authoritarian corporatism and socioeconomic dualism, they would have to be nurtured and sponsored by established elites.

The creation of industrial community requires an enhanced sense of involvement and social inclusion in the emerging industrial society at symbolic, material, and political levels. Symbolic inclusion refers to a sense that one's efforts and role are valued by the larger community, that one counts, and that one's work possesses some degree of meaning to oneself and others. Material inclusion relates not so much to levels of wages, benefits, and levels of living, as to equity, or the sense that the fruits of industry are being fairly distributed, as well as to feelings of material security and perhaps, in some cases, of proprietorship as well. Political inclusion refers to that sense of industrial citizenship which comes from control over one's work environment and participation or influence in economic decision making.

The symbolic inclusion of Singapore's blue-collar workers has involved an attempt to enhance the social status of manual labor. During the 1960s, and even into the early 1970s, Lee Kuan Yew often referred to Singapore's workers as "digits," a term suggestive of the generally accepted symbolic role of labor defined in terms of manpower needs and economic skills. Such cultural marginalization of manual workers, in part reflecting a general Chinese cultural repugnance to manual labor, was replaced during the 1970s by a new image of manual workers as important builders of modern Singapore. Increasingly, officials and union leaders derided male workers who opted for "cushy" white-collar jobs in airconditioned offices in lieu of hard manual labor. And a "work with your hands" campaign was launched in 1976 to emphasize the importance and value of such work. The campaign was kicked off by Lee Kuan Yew with the following words: "We must hold fast to the tried and trusted virtue of hard work: dirtying one's hands, sweating and soiling one's clothes are good for the body and soul, and for our economy" (quoted in Labour News 5/76).

If symbolic inclusion refers in part to a perception that one's work commands dignity and respect, it also relates to a feeling that one's work is meaningful and fits into a larger ordered whole. Starting from this assumption, the NTUC launched a campaign in 1978 to encourage workers to learn more about their firms in order to gain a stronger sense of organizational loyalty. The rationale for this "Get to know your company or industry" campaign was described by Secretary-General Devan Nair as follows:

> The most important element, from our point of view, is the Japanese concept that if workers and managers are to identify themselves with the companies they work for, and develop a strong sense of mutual belonging, they must be informed and educated about the special economics of the undertaking, the why and the wherefore of production or of servicing, as the case may be (The Straits Times 6/24/78).

Foreign companies themselves have in many cases tried to enhance worker loyalty through essentially symbolic means. For example, several Japanese firms have imported elements of their home employment practices into Singapore and rely on joint morning exercises, the singing of company songs, and recitations of company objectives in order to instill greater loyalty in workers. In addition, they are more likely than other foreign firms to deemphasize status differences within the firm, to give varied work assignments and continued training so that employees can move to higher levels, and to try to transfer workers with poor performance records before dismissing them (Tan Chuan Lye 1976).

The question of material inclusion of labor in Singapore's emerging industrial order is more problematic. It was noted that the evidence on income inequality is mixed. On the other hand, and perhaps more important than actual income equalization, however, has been the creation of an ever more comprehensive welfare state, the basis for Singapore's claim to "socialist" credentials. Public provision of low-cost housing, education, and medical and other social services has disproportionately benefited lower income groups (Chen 1975) thus substantially reducing otherwise large social class differences in living standards.

In addition, the material security of workers has been increased through passage of the Workers' Compensation Acts of 1971 and 1975 that include retrenchment benefits for workers laid off because of changed economic conditions. Security has also been enhanced through increased pressure on employers to provide for worker safety and by increased Ministry of Labour intervention on behalf of workers subject to unfair treatment at the hands of employers. Individual companies, too, have moved to enhance employee loyalty through various forms of company paternalism. National Semi-conductor is typical of many large electronics firms in its provision of recreational facilities, films, counseling services, loans, and even housing for some workers (Chua Ah Moy 1973).

Finally, the government has very recently introduced a drastic change in wage policy through acceptance of large wage increases over a period of several years for lower income groups (Goh 1979). While the official rationale for the new wage policy centers on a desire to induce technological upgrading and economic restructuring in the light of growing labor shortages, it has the additional consequence of narrowing income inequalities and thus perhaps of enhancing work morale and commitment as well. The new policy signals recognition of a point made some years ago by Wilbert Moore:

> Even from the individual employer's point of view,
> cheap labor may turn out to be rather expensive, owing to the vicious circle linking low wages and low
> productivity. Given any kind of market orientation on
> the part of workers, uneconomically high wages may be
> the correct transitional strategy (1965, p. 43).

MATERIAL INCLUSION AND THE NTUC COOPERATIVE MOVEMENT

Authoritarian corporatism is far more than just centralized domination of an atomistic public. It also seeks to stabilize such domination through structures which coopt potential opponents, provide information to the center, and provide an instrumentality for carrying out policy decisions. Most important in this regard is the national trade union structure, whose "productionist" role is of vital importance to the success of elite policies relating to the workforce and industrial relations. In Singapore's case, it has been largely through the NTUC structure that government has hoped to control and discipline the workforce, implement its incomes policy, and socialize workers to the values of hard work, sacrifice, and national loyalty.

In the context of declining union membership during the late 1960s, it was clear that only a revitalized union structure could effectively meet its productionist roles vis-a-vis national development goals. In order to achieve such revitalization, a variety of incentives and sanctions have been employed to increase membership and participation. First, government and NTUC officials have stressed that NWC recommendations are only bargainable by registered unions (The Straits Times 3/23/73). Similarly, only organized workers can submit disputes to IAC arbitration. Finally, government has established a dues checkoff system which has been introduced by many employers.

But far more important was the change in union orientation following a 1969 Seminar on the "Modernization of Labor," attended by Lee Kuan Yew and other government leaders, along with union officials and delegates. At this seminar, Goh Keng Swee, then Minister of Finance, suggested that the ailing unions become active in setting up worker cooperatives and social services. While direct government financial assistance was not offered, new legislation was enacted to permit unions to use internal funds for cooperative ventures, and government support and training were made available. The rationale for this change in union orientation, according to Goh, was to permit the NTUC to increase its influence over labor as well as its capacity to act as a channel for new programs. In response to Goh's suggestion, the NTUC, and particularly its largest affiliate, the Singapore Industrial Labour Organization, launched a massive cooperative program in such areas as food retailing, dental and health care, books and stationery, travel services, public transport and taxis, consumer protection, finance, and insurance. The cooperative movement, patterned after the Scandinavian model, has grown into a major social institution in Singapore. This movement provides an instrumental basis for increased union participation through the many benefits made available to members. In addition, it is intended to encourage loyalty based on a sense of coownership. Lee Kuan Yew has recognized the importance of this latter aspect of cooperatives:

> It is the consciousness of our being co-owners of the new society we are creating that provides the drive for fulfillment. In multi-racial countries like ours, trade unions have a special role in building up this spirit of camaraderie amongst the workers (quoted in Nair 1976, p. 97).

> Every citizen . . . feels he has a stake, a sense of proprietorship, in the stability and progress of Singapore (Far Eastern Economic Review 5/26/78).

This sentiment has been echoed by Devan Nair as well:

Trade unions and their members have therefore come
to possess a sense of belonging to their society and
their nation. They recognize that they are, in a very
real and tangible sense, the co-owners of society
(Nair 1976, pp. 102-3).

The seriousness with which government takes the cooperative movement is shown by the recent infusion of civil servants and Members
of Parliament into advisory positions in cooperatives and unions,
and the presence of high-level government officials on the boards of
directors of some cooperative enterprises.

Following the success of the cooperative movement, the NTUC
has more recently launched a new organization, the Labour Foundation, mandated to reach beyond workers themselves to provide legal,
training, educational, child care, welfare, and other services to
workers' families. This new phase, as yet only in its infancy, has
been dubbed the "socialization and humanization phase" of the labor
movement (Gan 1976). Related to this new initiative was the government's decision to transfer control over day care centers from
the Ministry of Social Affairs to the NTUC (The Straits Times
7/28/78), and to establish a separate NTUC secretariat for welfare
and community services which will focus on the welfare needs of
workers and their families and the involvement of workers in community development programs (Singapore Economic Bulletin 4/80,
p. 55).

POLITICAL INCLUSION: THE LIMITS
OF CORPORATIST PARTICIPATION

In an insightful discussion of Singapore's massive public housing program, Hassan points out that "a disturbing feature is that
while a large number of Singaporeans willingly form a major component of the resources being mobilized, they appear to exhibit only
limited commitment to the new environment which this mobilization
is fashioning for them" (Hassan 1976, p. 345). Noting the lack of
public involvement in the maintenance and upkeep of housing units,
he attributes these and other manifestations óf weak commitment to
lack of participation in the program (p. 344).

One attempt to enhance such participation has involved the operation of community centers and tenants' committees throughout
the city. Today there are 175 community centers through which are
organized recreational, cultural, vocational, educational, and community extension programs and services along with exhibitions,

displays, talks, film shows, and discussion forums (Wong and Chen 1977). The centers, along with a large number of other social, cultural, and educational associations, are in turn governed by the Peoples' Association, a statutory board mandated to "perform the dual functions of providing avenues of mobilization and political participation for the people and at the same time socializing the participants to accept basic values aimed at creating a consensual political base in the country" (quoted in Chan 1976, p. 44). The problematic combination of corporatist goals of socialization on the one hand and popular participation on the other has been noted by Seah (1973) and has been cited as a contributing cause of low levels of community involvement or interest in center activities (Hassan 1976, p. 343).

Corresponding problems of tenuous institutional commitment in the industrial workforce have in part been addressed through greater emphasis on at least symbolic forms of decision-making participation by workers. Of particular significance has been the introduction of human relations programs in individual firms and the expansion of "tripartite" union participation in enterprise and national-level economic decision making.

There has been increasing official and managerial recognition of the need for improved work morale (Josey 1976, p. 4), especially in higher technology industries which require initiative and responsibility in workers. Thus, foreign management in particular has begun to introduce, in a new setting, human relations practices long accepted at home. Illustrative of such efforts is the job-enrichment and workteam program at one large U.S.-based electronics firm in Singapore. The firm has set up teams of coworkers and their supervisors to jointly work out methods of improving productivity and work standards. Teams which come up with particularly good ideas receive prizes and recognition awards.

Tripartism in Singapore refers to joint economic decision making by employers, unions, and government at national and enterprise levels. Its antecedents go back to the 1965 Charter for Progress, discussed earlier, as well as to early labor representation on such public bodies as the Economic Development Board, the Housing and Development Board, and the Industrial Arbitration Court. But tripartism was greatly extended through the creation, in 1972, of the National Wages Council, consisting of delegates from government, employers, and the NTUC. Through NWC participation, labor is represented in the yearly formulation of general guidelines for wage increases, wage structure, and incentive schemes to be implemented in collective agreements. The socially integrative rationale for such tripartite representation of labor was suggested in Lee Kuan Yew's 1978 May Day speech. There, he spoke of the need, through the NTUC, to "create a series of overlapping and

reinforcing organic links through which every worker identifies him-
self directly with nation-building. . . . Only because they [workers]
were organized in unions, with union leaders being identified in the
big decisions which have shaped the new Singapore, so we today have
a body of workers who feel themselves a part of Singapore's organic
whole" (The Straits Times 5/1/78).

Tripartism at the level of the individual enterprise has been
encouraged through the formation of works councils. This idea,
given special attention in 1973 at an NTUC-organized symposium
which affirmed unions' status as "partners in production within an
integral society," has as yet generated little enthusiasm or participation from employers.

Material and symbolic forms of social inclusion of the industrial workforce are fully compatible with authoritarian corporatism
so long as they are accomplished within an essentially paternalistic
framework. More problematic is the relationship between participation and corporatism, since such participation must challenge
neither basic policy nor the right of ruling elites to create and implement such a policy at their own discretion. By consequence,
corporatist participation is not only channeled through "authorita-
tively-sanctioned interest associations" (Malloy 1977), but is also
confined to lower-level decisions or problems of policy implementation rather than of basic policy formulation and is largely informa-
tional or advisory.

Tripartite participation by labor in Singapore's economic decision making at national and enterprise levels is limited in scope
and corporatist in structure and ideology. At the national level,
NWC recommendations are advisory only. Government is free to
amend or even reject the recommendations altogether, although unacceptable recommendations are unlikely to be presented. The
NTUC delegates who participate in NWC deliberations are high-level
officials in what has been a tightly centralized and politically integrated labor federation, thus reducing the extent of rank-and-file
interest representation. Such deliberations are institutionally re-
mote both from the workers whose interests they are to take into
account and from the actual wage determination process which occurs at the enterprise level. Finally, such participation takes place
within an ideological milieu which discourages the expression of
basic disagreement with established development policies. This
was made clear in a speech by the Minister of Labor in 1973, in
which he emphasized the "fundamental identity of interests between
workers and management, and the higher loyalty of both to national,
vs. sectional interests" (Josey 1976, p. 4). Partly in recognition
of the difficulties of meaningful participation in a highly centralized
trade union structure, Devan Nair announced in 1980 replacement of

SILO and PIEU with smaller industry-based unions (Singapore Economic Bulletin 4/80, p. 55). As of this writing, the future of this new decentralization effort is uncertain.

Similarly limited has been participation in enterprise-level decision making through works councils. By 1973, only six such councils had been set up (The Straits Times 12/12/73). Such lack of employer enthusiasm for works councils probably stems from the global rather than local nature of management policy making in multinational firms, as well as the fact that such councils would intrude upon already established managerial prerogatives in such areas as work organization and allocation (Pang and Kay 1974). In discussing the NTUC's 1973 call for greater national commitment to the roles of both management and unions as "co-partners in production," Pang Eng Fong, a leading authority on labor and industrial relations in Singapore, has commented: "A fundamental revision of the 1968 labour laws is needed if unions are to participate in plant decision making to the extent implied by [this] term . . ." (Pang and Kay 1974).

Given the importance of the NTUC from the standpoints both of productionist roles and social integration, how successful have been recent efforts to revitalize and strengthen the national union structure? In 1976, NTUC Secretary-General Devan Nair asserted that:

> As a result of the wide-ranging scope and thrust of
> trade union interests, projects, and programmes,
> and of direct trade union involvement in the decision-
> making processes of key areas of socio-economic plan-
> ning and development, the labour movement has ac-
> quired a status and influence in the public life of the
> nation, unheard of in most parts of the developing,
> and, indeed, even in many developed countries. Trade
> unions and their members have therefore come to pos-
> sess a sense of belonging to their society and their
> nation (Nair 1976, pp. 102-3).

While Nair's conclusions are perhaps overstated, Table 5.1 does suggest a remarkable and continuing union membership increase after 1970, the year of the launching of the cooperative movement. And, significantly, the most spectacular membership increases were in SILO, the national union which was most active in setting up cooperative ventures (The Straits Times 4/25/73).

CONCLUSION: THE EMERGING
CORPORATE PATERNALISM

Singapore is well past the earlier period of economic and political repression of labor so essential to the consolidation of PAP rule and the initial encouragement of industrial investment. It has increasingly become a moral community in which a largely paternalistic government protects workers from employer exploitation, provides for their material needs, and affirms the dignity of their labor. The legitimacy of the ruling elite derives in part from basic principles of Confucian moral philosophy (Geiger 1972), and in larger measure from its successful development policies which have provided jobs and the economic basis for a modern welfare state.

In the context of growing socioeconomic complexity accompanying rapid industrialization, the state depends to an ever greater degree on mechanisms not only to control popular groups, but to provide for the upward communication of needs and grievances as well. While tripartite worker participation in economic decision making may seem insignificant by the standards of Western, pluralist models of autonomous interest representation, it does provide an important, if limited, channel for the upward flow of information essential to the functioning of Singapore's corporate paternalist political order.

7
SUMMARY AND CONCLUSIONS

The earlier literature on social institutional aspects of industrialization started from the essentially functionalist question: what
are the most important institutional requirements for the functioning
of a modern industrial society (Moore 1965, p. 28)? Having once
established these requirements, analysis turned to the problematic
issue of worker commitment to new industrial norms and organizations. While such an approach is very useful in suggesting important areas of change accompanying industrialization, it allows one
largely to ignore the historical processes through which new institutions are created, as well as important cross-national or cross-
cultural differences in the nature of emerging industrial institutions
and organizations. By consequence, it fails to address the structural complexities of economic and political change, or the ramifications of different modes of change for the social order or the individual. In this study, we have directly confronted these problems
in the context of an increasingly common industrialization strategy
based in part on the political assurance of readily available, productive, disciplined, and low-cost labor in order to attract foreign capital investment in export oriented, labor-absorbing manufacturing.
Such a combination of authoritarian corporatism in state-labor relations on one hand and world market oriented industrialization on the
other is most pronounced and of greatest social consequence in such
rapidly industrializing societies as Singapore, South Korea, and to a
lesser extent Taiwan. Thus, this development pattern and its social
ramifications may most readily be observed in those societies.
But the study of such an industrialization strategy acquires a
broader significance when it is realized that many other third world
countries are trying to emulate the remarkable economic success of

these Asian societies in their own industrial development planning, as suggested by the widespread creation of export-processing industrial estates. While the industrial sector in such countries may comprise a smaller segment of the national economy, one might anticipate many of the same social and political consequences there, although they would be less visible by virtue of being submerged in broader and more complex processes of social change.

On the basis of the case study of singapore, several general propositions may be offered. These propositions should be taken only as suggestive of possibly fruitful starting points for further comparative research on the industrialization process in third world countries.

1. The greater the reliance on labor-intensive industrialization as the basis for national economic development and the reduction of unemployment, the greater the tendency to impose authoritarian corporatist controls over labor in order to enhance its productivity, discipline, and low-cost availability to potential investors.

Singapore, Korea, and Taiwan are small countries with limited domestic markets, few resources, and, in the first two cases, minimal agricultural potential. On the other hand, they all entered their periods of rapid economic growth with an overabundance of workers who were acquisitive, partially urbanized, and highly responsive to wage incentives. Under these circumstances, development planning in all three cases turned naturally to an export oriented growth strategy based on labor-intensive industry. And, from the beginning, the efficient upgrading, utilization, and discipline of human resources became the touchstone of development success. In each of these countries, the state has made massive human capital investments in education, housing, and public health. But, conversely, it has imposed tight corporatist controls on unions in order to stabilize labor costs and to enhance labor productivity and industrial stability.

If size and resource considerations dictated a strategy of labor-intensive, export oriented industrialization, several important political and other preconditions have ensured the successful adoption of such a strategy. All three countries started their periods of rapid industrialization with strong, unified ruling elites within dominant, single-party systems. The power of these elites, which permitted them to control labor and subdue political opposition, derived, to varying degrees, from unifying external threats, low levels of political mobilization, and the absence of independent and dynamic professional or entrepreneurial classes. In addition, the countries are small and relatively undifferentiated, thus facilitating centralized political control.

This unique set of economic constraints and political preconditions generated very similar growth strategies in these countries, based on authoritarian corporatism and world market oriented manufacturing.

2. The labor cost stabilization, industrial peace, and political stability resulting from effective authoritarian corporatist controls over organized labor combine with other incentives and locational factors to determine the extent of attraction of international capital into world market oriented manufacturing. Such investment, in turn, provides the basis for rapid industrial development and employment generation.

It was noted that imposition during the late 1960s of tight labor controls both in Singapore and Korea was associated with a subsequent rapid expansion of foreign investment in labor-absorbing manufacturing. Similarly, Taiwan's rapid industrialization has been based heavily on foreign, export oriented manufacturing investment in labor-intensive industries.

3. World market oriented industrialization has several socioeconomic consequences which tend further to buttress and consolidate political authoritarian corporatism. These consequences are as follows:

a. The creation of an increasingly ineffectual and dependent local bourgeoisie unable to effectively challenge ruling elites. In Singapore, domestic private enterprise is either relatively stagnant or, alternately, increasingly dependent upon foreign business enterprise. In South Korea and Taiwan, local businessmen have played a somewhat more active entrepreneurial role in industrialization than in Singapore in part because of their greater direct involvement in subcontracted export-manufacture,* but they too have been largely dependent upon government for access to foreign capital. In all three societies domestic economic elites lack an independent resource base for political action.

b. The weakening of local politically autonomous community structures. This happens in part because of a decline in the economic base for community institutions and in part because of a shift from local to outside economic opportunities, especially for young persons newly entering the labor market. In Singapore, this shift has been associated with increasing student enrollments in English-stream, vocationally oriented education, growing outside

---

*Robert Snow 1980: personal observation.

social contacts, and increasing outmarriage. In the Korean and Taiwanese cases, community disruption has primarily taken the form of an exodus of young female workers from rural areas to industrial estates.

c. The generation of an expanding resource base for ruling elites in heavily foreign-invested economic activities. Of particular importance is the political neutrality of the source of much new government revenue which increases the independence of political elites vis-a-vis local interest groups.

Industrial expansion has in part made possible massive government investments in social infrastructure, particularly in Singapore and Taiwan. Such investments, in housing, education, and public health have substantially raised national standards of living despite continuing wage controls. And industrialization has been associated not with increasing income inequality, as suggested by dependency theorists, but by a modest narrowing of income gaps (Pang 1975; Kim and Halpern 1977, p. 31; McBeath 1978) in large part because of the magnitude of employment generation in all three countries. In these ways rapid industrialization has legitimated and underwritten authoritarian corporatist rule.

d. Simplification of the economic structure through diversion of economic resources and labor into a few key export industries. This reduces the complexity of the trade union movement and facilitates its consolidation into a centralized, corporatist structure.

e. Atomization of the workforce, the result of changes both in the employment context and in workforce composition. The majority of workers in world market oriented manufacturing in all three societies experience low job security, lack of advancement opportunity, impersonal labor controls, low wages, and overwhelming, politically backed, managerial authority (Frobel et al 1980, III). In addition, the workforce is characterized by large numbers of young, female, and economically marginal groups. These two sets of factors, which together suggest a disproportionate expansion of the secondary employment sector, tend to reduce solidarity among workers, and thus the capacity for effective worker opposition to political authoritarianism as well.

4. World market oriented industrialization in the context of authoritarian corporatist state-labor relations is associated with a progressive demoralization of the industrial workforce and with continuing problems of tenuous and expediency-based worker commitment to industrial institutions, norms, and organizations. Such problems have already been discussed in the context of Korea and Singapore and apply as well to Taiwan's export oriented industrial sectors, particularly in the free export zones, which exhibit high

rates of labor turnover, apathy, and absenteeism (Wall Street Journal 9/2/76).

Huntington (1968), Duvall and Welfling (1973), and others have discussed the negative institutional consequences of a more rapid mobilization of interest groups and popular aspirations than can be accommodated by established political institutions. A successful corporatist system like that of South Korea or Singapore, on the other hand, suggests precisely the opposite problem. Singapore's pervasive authoritarian corporatism, along with the rapid world market oriented industrialization it has made possible, is associated not with under-institutionalization, but rather with hyper-institutionalization, or the elaboration of institutional controls which both outrun and destroy their necessary sociocultural anchorage. While rapid economic growth and a rising standard of living may enhance material satisfactions, alienative and highly expedient institutional and organizational commitments pose longer run threats to continued development and stability. First, weak expedient attachment to firms is economically disruptive. Second, expedient political support implies a heightened vulnerability to economic fluctuations. Open industrial economies such as those of Singapore, Korea, and Taiwan are highly responsive to changes in levels of international market demand by virtue of their export concentration in a few major industries. The 1974-75 world recession, for example, led to the layoff of thousands of workers in the major export oriented industries of these societies and generated a marked increase in forms of labor protest which were in violation of established labor and industrial relations laws. Such protests were, of course, disorganized and easily contained and, in any case, declined rapidly with the post-1975 resumption of growth. Nevertheless, they did dramatize the need for deeper moral and social commitments among workers.

Third, in Singapore's case, tenuous attachments to NTUC-affiliated unions undercut their productionist roles relating to wage restraint, productivity, discipline, sacrifice, and loyalty to firms, as well as their ability to integrate workers into the industrial and political community and to mobilize worker support for national development policies.

5. The corporatist dilemma between the needs for control on one hand and commitment on the other generates pressure on political elites to move toward increasingly popular modes of authoritarian corporatism. Bureaucratic-authoritarian corporatist controls lead to the attenuation of social bonds and commitments in industry. The resulting labor force demoralization, however, encourages attempts to revitalize such bonds, especially relating to firms and unions.

The crucial role of political elites in such revitalization follows from several characteristics of the new industrialization pattern which differentiate it from other historical patterns. There is, of course, nothing new in the social disorganizational consequences of rapid industrialization. Factory managers in nineteenth-century Britain, like their twentieth-century industrial successors in Singapore, had to contend with similar problems of low commitment and high turnover. In both cases, such problems were caused by many of the same factors, including rapid industrial change, new socially isolating technologies, and the entry of new groups into industrial employment. And in both cases, too, institutional innovation initially outran the crystallization and adaptation of stabilizing social bonds and cultural commitments.

The new pattern does differ from other cases, however, in the respect that authoritarian corporatism and world market oriented industrialization have effectively demobilized the social bases for the autonomous emergence of a stable social order. Industrial community building in Singapore and South Korea cannot start from existing social or cultural identities, nor, in the context of authoritarian corporatism, can it emerge through the institutionalization of conflict among autonomous economic interest groups. If community is to emerge at all, it will have to be a creation of the state.

In part, the revitalization of social bonds in industry can be accomplished through incentives and value appeals. But a further requirement is that workers experience a greater sense of participation in and control over economic decisions and policies which affect them. To maintain authoritarian corporatist controls over labor, elites must channel such participation through authoritatively sanctioned structures and confine it to intermediate levels of decision making. And, most importantly from the standpoints both of control and legitimacy, participation must take place within an essentially paternalistic framework: one, that is, in which elites respond adequately and fairly, but at their own discretion, to interest representation which takes the form of petition, advice, or information, rather than of political demand. Such political paternalism greatly extends and amplifies the legitimating consequences of material and symbolic forms of paternalism, and thus lends stability to an increasingly popular authoritarian corporatism which permits elites simultaneously to pursue the otherwise incompatible goals of social mobilization and control (Schoutz 1978).

Neither South Korea nor Taiwan have directly or effectively addressed problems of labor demoralization, although Taiwan has initiated a "New Community Movement," whose goal is to provide a spiritual basis for industrial life based on piety to superiors, teamwork, and paternalistic labor-management relations. Singapore has been the only one of these countries to systematically build the national trade union structure into an instrument not only of production but of social integration as well. And it is noteworthy that the Singapore government must rely on police controls to a far lesser degree than the governments of either South Korea or Taiwan.

Dependency theory has largely been based on studies of large, agrarian societies whose economies have increasingly been dominated by foreign investment in capital-intensive, extractive, and industrial activities. The socioeconomic consequences of such a development pattern, it is often argued, include a lopsided economic structure, economic structural de-differentiation, enclave development or economic regression, income inequality, and the emergence of "compradore" political and economic elites.

The application by Frobel of a dependency perspective to the recent, more labor-intensive pattern of world market oriented industrialization suggests the further sociopolitical consequences of increased wage controls, union repression, and social atomism in the industrial workforce. These latter consequences, it should be noted, are largely confined to the typically rather small manufacturing export zones of developing societies.

But what happens when world market oriented industrialization becomes the dominant feature of the total national economy? Such a possibility, which is especially relevant for small societies with few exploitable natural and agricultural resources and where elites have successfully centered their development strategy on a marriage of local labor with foreign manufacturing capital, would suggest an amplification of the social consequences discussed by Frobel as well as the possibility of qualitative differences in such consequences because of their broader systemic ramifications.

Frobel suggests that in the case of Singapore, virtually the whole territory functions as a free production zone for export oriented manufacturing. This implies that Singapore may comprise a limiting case of the social ramifications of world market oriented industrialization which would occur to a lesser degree in other small societies (for example, Korea and Taiwan) which are pursuing similar development strategies.

Singapore suggests several major departures from the older dependency model: a generalization of corporatist modes of political control from industrial enclaves to the larger political society; an expansion not only in national income, but in employment as well, sufficient to reduce economic inequality and greatly increase material standards of living; and a diminution in the political influence of multinational firms over local political elites because of growing competition among firms and increasing diversification in the nationalities of major foreign investors (Kassalow 1978). In addition, it raises the possibility of growing pressure toward state-sponsored social mobilization within a popular-authoritarian form of political corporatism in order to reduce the ever more apparent problem of economic and political demoralization.

It suggests that successful world market oriented industrialization may be associated not with political liberalization but rather with continuing authoritarianism. In part, this is the result of continuing dependent, dualistic development in the context of increasing efforts to attract higher technology industries. The only major alternative to such dependency would be rapid expansion in state economic enterprise. But in the case of Singapore, there exist two longer-term economic problems whose solutions may carry the society further down the road of increasing political authoritarianism. The first of these problems is the growing wage-trap, or upward pressure on wages resulting from full employment and rising living costs in an urban society. Short of an upgrading of technology and skills sufficiently rapid to keep pace with recent wage increases, the continuing competition for offshore investment posed by neighboring labor-surplus economies may increase the need for political controls over wages and other labor costs. Second, Singapore's vulnerability to world export market fluctuations and recession heightens the need for political controls sufficient to contain economic protest during periods of economic slowdown. Given the improbability that Singapore's recent remarkable economic growth rates can continue forever, this problem will probably be a recurrent one.

Singapore's dramatic economic success has not been without substantial cost in human and social dislocation and political discipline. Yet given Singapore's growing economic crisis during the 1960s, there were probably few alternatives to the development strategy adopted by the PAP. Assuming continuing political stability and economic growth, the remaining questions relate to the ability of political elites to nurture those social and cultural commitments which will transform Singapore's modern economy into a more human community as well.

BIBLIOGRAPHY

Adelman, Irma, and S. Robinson. Income Distribution Policy in Developing Countries: A Case Study of Korea. Stanford, Cal.: Stanford University Press, 1978.

Ahmad, Sharifah. "Japanese Manufacturing Establishments in Singapore." Unpublished academic exercise, Department of Economics, University of Singapore, 1975.

Apter, David. "Charters, Cartels, and Multinationals—Some Colonial and Imperial Questions." In The Multinational Corporation and Social Change, edited by David Apter and Louis Goodman. New York: Praeger, 1976.

Awbery, S. S., and F. W. Dalley. Labour and Trade Union Organization in the Federation of Malaya and Singapore. Kuala Lampur: Government Press, 1948.

Baran, P. A. The Political Economy of Growth. New York: Monthly Review Press, 1957.

Bates, Robert. "Approaches to the Study of Unions and Development." Industrial Relations 9 (1970).

Bellows, Thomas. "Taiwan's Foreign Policy in the 1970's: A Case Study of Adaptation and Viability." Asian Survey 16 (1976): 593-611.

Belshaw, Cyril. Traditional Exchange and Modern Markets. Englewood Cliffs, N.J.: Prentice-Hall, 1965.

Bendix, Reinhard. Work and Authority in Industry. New York: Harper & Row, 1956.

Bingham, R. P. Report of the Singapore Labour Department, 1946. Singapore: Government Printing Office, 1947.

Blau, Peter. Exchange and Power in Social Life. New York: Wiley, 1964.

Blythe, W. L. "Historical Sketch of Chinese Labour in Malaya." Royal Asiatic Society Journal 20 (June 1947).

Buchanan, Iain. Singapore in Southeast Asia. London: G. Bell & Sons, 1972.

Carstens, Sharon. Chinese Associations in Singapore Society. Singapore: Institute of Southeast Asian Studies, 1975.

Chalmers, Douglas. "The Politicized State in Latin America." In Authoritarianism and Corporatism in Latin America, edited by James Malloy. Pittsburgh: University of Pittsburgh, 1977.

Chalmers, W. E. Critical Issues in Industrial Relations in Singapore. Singapore: Donald Moore Press, 1967.

Chalmers, W. E., and Pang Eng Fong. "Industrial Relations." In Modern Singapore, edited by Ooi Jin-Bee and Chiang Hai Ding. Singapore: University of Singapore Press, 1969.

Chan Heng Chee. "Politics in an Administrative State." In Trends in Singapore, edited by Seah Chee Meow, pp. 51-68. Singapore: University of Singapore Press, 1975.

_____. "The Political System and Political Change." In Singapore: Society in Transition, edited by Riaz Hassan, pp. 30-51. Kuala Lampur: Oxford University Press, 1976.

Chang Chen Tung. "The Changing Socio-Demographic Profile." In Singapore: Society in Transition, edited by Riaz Hassan, pp. 271-89. Kuala Lampur: Oxford University Press, 1976.

Chang Kung Yee. "A Study of Fifteen Young Singaporean Chinese Male Factory Workers Living in Dormitory Flats in Jurong." Unpublished academic exercise, Department of Social Work, University of Singapore, 1973.

Chaplin, D. "Blue-Collar Workers in Peru." International Journal of Comparative Sociology 10 (1969).

Chase-Dunn, Christopher. "The Effects of International Economic Dependence on Development and Inequality: A Cross-National Study." American Sociological Review 40 (1975).

Chen, Peter S. J. "The Political Course of Singapore." Department of Sociology, University of Singapore, Working Papers, 1972.

_____. "Growth and Income Distribution in Singapore." Unpublished manuscript, Department of Sociology, University of Singapore, 1975.

Cheng, Lean Kiow. "A Comparison Between the Modern and Traditional Management Practices in Singapore." Unpublished academic exercise, Department of Economics, University of Singapore, 1968.

Chew Ooi Ai. "The Bataks in Singapore: A Study of Group Cohesion and Assimilation." Unpublished Masters Thesis, Department of Sociology, University of Singapore, 1978.

Chia, S. Y. "Growth and Pattern of Industrialization." In The Singapore Economy, edited by Yon Poh Seng and Lim Chiong Yah. Singapore: Eastern Universities Press, 1971.

Chiang See Ngoh, Claire. "The Hainanese Community of Singapore." Unpublished academic exercise, Department of Sociology, University of Singapore, 1977.

Chua Ah Moy. "A Study of Twenty Factory Girls." Unpublished academic exercise, Department of Social Work, University of Singapore, 1973.

Coch, Lester, and R. French, Jr. "Overcoming Resistance to Change." Human Relations 11 (1948): 512-32.

Cohen, Benjamin. Multinational Firms and Asian Exports. New Haven, Conn.: Yale University Press, 1975.

Cole, David, and Princeton Lyman. Korean Development. Cambridge, Mass.: Harvard University Press, 1971.

Cole, G. D. H. "The Emergence and Nature of Trade Unions." In Man, Work, and Society, edited by Sigmund Nosow and William Form, pp. 176-84. New York: Basic Books, 1962.

Cole, Robert E. "The Theory of Institutionalization: Permanent Employment and Tradition in Japan." Economic Development and Cultural Change 20 (1971): 47-70.

Collier, David, and Ruth Collier. "Who Does What, to Whom, and How: Toward a Comparative Analysis of Latin American Corporatism." In Authoritarianism and Corporatism in Latin America, edited by James Malloy. Pittsburgh: University of Pittsburgh, 1977

Conquest, Robert. Industrial Workers in the U.S.S.R. New York: Praeger, 1967.

Cooley, Charles. Social Organization. New York: Scribner's, 1909.

Cordova, Efren. "Labour Legislation and Latin American Development: A Preliminary Review." International Labour Review 106 (1972).

Coser, Lewis. The Functions of Social Conflict. London: Routledge, 1956.

_____. Continuities in the Study of Social Conflict. New York: Free Press, 1967.

Dahrendorf, Ralf. Class and Class Conflict in Industrial Society. London: Routledge and Kegan Paul, 1959.

Dalton, Melville. Men Who Manage. New York: Wiley, 1959.

Delacroix, Jacques, and Charles Ragin. "Modernizing Institutions, Mobilization, and Third-World Development: A Cross-national Study." American Journal of Sociology 84 (July 1978): 123-50.

Deutsch, Karl. "Social Mobilization and Political Development." American Political Science Review 55 (September 1961): 493-511.

Deyo, Frederic. "Ethnicity and Work Culture in Thailand." Journal of Asian Studies 34 (August 1975): 995-1015.

_____. "Local Foremen in Multinational Enterprise." Journal of Management Studies 15 (October 1978): 308-17.

_____. "The Single Female Factory Worker and Her Peer Group." Human Organization 39 (Spring 1980).

Deyo, Frederic, and Peter Chen. "Female Labour-Force Participation and Earnings in Singapore." Economic Bulletin for Asia and the Pacific 27 (June 1976): 82-99.

Doraisamy, T. R., ed. 150 Years of Education in Singapore. Singapore: Teachers' Training College Publication Board, 1969.

Dubin, Robert. "Industrial Conflict and Social Welfare." Journal of Conflict Resolution 1 (June 1957): 179-99.

Dunlop, J. T. Industrial Relations Systems. New York: Holt, Rinehart, 1958.

Durkheim, Emile. The Division of Labor in Society. New York: Free Press, 1933.

Duvall, Raymond, and Mary Welfling. "Social Mobilization, Political Institutionalization, and Conflict in Black Africa." Journal of Conflict Resolution 17 (December 1973): 673-702.

Eisenstadt, S. N. "Social Institutions." In International Encyclopedia of the Social Sciences, edited by David Sills. New York: Free Press, 1968.

Eldridge, J. E. T. Sociology and Industrial Life. Cambridge, Mass.: Nelson, 1971.

_____. "Industrial Conflict: Some Problems of Theory and Method." In Man and Organization, edited by John Child. London: Allen & Unwin, 1973.

Etzioni, Amitai. Modern Organizations. Englewood Cliffs, N.J.: Prentice-Hall, 1964.

Feldman, Arnold, and Wilbert Moore. "The Market." In Labor Commitment and Social Change in Developing Areas, edited by Arnold Feldman and Wilbert Moore, Chapter 3. New York: Social Science Research Council, 1960.

Form, William. "Occupational and Social Integration of Automobile Workers in Four Countries: A Comparative Study." International Journal of Comparative Sociology 10 (1969).

Fox, Alan. A Sociology of Work in Industry. London: Collier-Macmillan, 1971.

_____. "Industrial Relations: A Social Critique of Pluralist Ideology." In Man and Organization, edited by John Child. London: Allen & Unwin, 1973.

Frank, A. G. Latin America: Underdevelopment or Revolution. New York: Monthly Review Press, 1972.

Friedland, William. Unions and Industrial Relations in Underdeveloped Countries. Ithaca: New York School of Industrial and Labor Relations, 1963.

_____. "Labor's Role in Emerging African Socialist States." In The Role of Labor in African Nation-Building, edited by Willard Beling. New York: Praeger, 1968.

Frobel, F., Jurgen Heinrichs, and Otto Kreye. The New International Division of Labor. New York: Cambridge University Press. Part III (1980).

Furtado, Celso. Economic Development of Latin America. Cambridge, Mass.: Cambridge University Press, 1970.

Galenson, Walter. "Introduction." In Labor in Developing Economics, edited by W. Galenson. Berkeley: University of California Press, 1962.

Galtung, Johan. "A Structural Theory of Imperialism." Journal of Peace Research 8 (1971).

Gamba, Charles. The Origins of Trade Unionism in Malaya. Singapore: Eastern Universities Press, 1962.

Gamer, Robert. The Politics of Urban Development in Singapore. Ithaca, N.Y.: Cornell University Press, 1972.

Gan, Delice. "The Changing Role of the Singapore National Trades Union Congress in National Development." Unpublished academic exercise, Department of Sociology, University of Singapore, 1976.

Geertz, Clifford. "The Integrative Revolution: Primordial Sentiments and Civil Politics in the New States." In Old Societies and New States, edited by Clifford Geertz. New York: Free Press, 1963.

Geiger, Theodore. Tales of Two City-States: The Development Progress of Hong Kong and Singapore. Washington, D.C.: National Planning Association, 1973.

Goh, Chok Tong. "Industrial Growth: 1959-66." In Modern Singapore, edited by Ooi Jin-Bee and Chiang Hai Ding. Singapore: University of Singapore, 1969.

_____. "Restructuring the Economy Through Higher Wages." Speech delivered at 47th annual dinner of The Singapore Manufacturers' Association, Neptune Theatre Restaurant, June 29, 1979.

Grodzins, Morton. The Loyal and the Disloyal: Social Boundaries of Patriotism and Treason. Chicago: University of Chicago Press, 1956.

Hanna, Willard. Success and Sobriety in Singapore. American Universities Field Staff, Southeast Asian Series, vol. 16, no. 2 (1968).

Harris, Richard. "The Political Economy of Africa: Underdevelopment or Revolution." In The Political Economy of Africa, edited by Richard Harris. Cambridge, Mass.: Schenkman, 1975.

Hasan, Parvez. Korea: Problems and Issues in a Rapidly Growing Economy. Baltimore: Johns Hopkins University Press, 1976.

Hassan, Riaz. "Symptoms and Syndrome of the Development Process." In Singapore: Society in Transition, edited by Riaz Hassan. Kuala Lampur: Oxford University Press, 1976.

Heyzer, Noeleen. "The Formation of an Industrial Workforce." Master's thesis, Department of Sociology, University of Singapore, 1974.

Heyzer, Noeleen, and Week Gek Sim. "Trade Union Leaders in Singapore." Department of Sociology, University of Singapore, Working Papers, 1972.

Ho Min Fong. "Woman [sic] Workers in Singapore Want a Fair Deal." Straits Times, 10/29/74.

Ho, Samuel. Economic Development of Taiwan: 1860-1970. New Haven, Conn.: Yale University Press, 1978.

Hoogvelt, Ankie. The Sociology of Developing Societies. London: Macmillan, 1976.

Hoselitz, Bert. Sociological Aspects of Economic Growth. New York: Free Press, 1960.

_____. "Tradition and Economic Growth." In Tradition, Values, and Socio-Economic Development, edited by Ralph Braibanti and Joseph Spengler, pp. 83-113. Durham, N.C.: Duke University Press, 1961.

_____. "The Development of a Labor Market in the Process of Economic Growth." In The International Labor Movement in Transition, edited by Adolf Sturmthal and James Scoville. Urbana: University of Illinois, 1973.

Huntington, Samuel. Political Order in Changing Societies. New Haven, Conn.: Yale University Press, 1968.

Ibrahim, Bibijan. "The Dawoodi Bohra Muslims: Ethnic Boundary Maintenance." Unpublished academic exercise, Department of Sociology, University of Singapore, 1977.

Ingham, Geoffrey. Strikes and Industrial Action. London: Macmillan, 1974.

International Labor Organization. Multinational Enterprises and Social Policy. Geneva: ILO, 1973.

Johnson, Caswell. "Political Unionism and the Collective Objective in Economies of British Colonial Origin: The Cases of Jamaica and Trinidad." American Journal of Economics and Sociology 34 (1975).

Johnson, Dale. "Dependence and the International System." In Dependence and Under-Development, edited by A. G. Frank and D. L. Johnson. New York: Anchor, 1972.

Josey, Alex. Lee Kuan Yew. Rev. ed. Singapore: Asia Pacific Press, 1971.

_____. Industrial Relations: Labour Laws in a Developing Singapore. Singapore: Federal Publications, 1976.

Kannappan, Subbiah. "Bargaining Theory and Developing Countries." In Industrial Relations: Contemporary Issues, edited by B. C. Roberts. New York: St. Martin's Press, 1968.

Kassalow, Everett. Trade Unions and Industrial Relations. New York: Random House, 1969.

_____. "Aspects of Labour Relations in Multinational Companies: An Overview of Three Asian Countries." International Labour Review 117 (1978): 273-87.

Kaufman, Robert. "Corporatism, Clientelism, and Partisan Conflict: A Study of Seven Latin American Countries." In Authoritarianism and Corporatism in Latin America, edited by James Malloy. Pittsburgh: University of Pittsburgh, 1977.

Kay, Thelma. "Group Cohesion and Productivity Among Dockworkers: A Study of Stevedores in Singapore." Department of Sociology, University of Singapore, Working Papers, no. 20 (1973).

Kaye, Barrington. Upper Nanking Street, Singapore: A Sociological Study of Chinese Households Living in a Densely Populated Area. Singapore: University of Malaya Press, 1960.

Kearney, Robert. Trade Unions and Politics in Ceylon. Berkeley: University of California Press, 1971.

Kerr, Clark, John Dunlop, Frederick Harbison, and Charles Meyers. Industrialism and Industrial Man. Cambridge, Mass.: Harvard University Press, 1960.

Kerr, Clark, and A. Siegel. "The Interindustry Propensity to Strike: An International Comparison." In Industrial Conflict, edited by A. Kornhauser et al. New York: McGraw-Hill, 1954.

Kesselman, Mark. "Overinstitutionalization and Political Constraint." Comparative Politics (October 1970): 21-44.

Kim, C. I. Eugene. "Emergency, Development, and Human Rights: South Korea." Asian Survey 18 (1978): 363-78.

Kim, Jungsae. "Recent Trends in the Government's Management of the Economy." In Korean Politics in Transition, edited by Edward Wright. Seattle: University of Washington Press, 1975.

Kim, Kyong-Dong. "Political Factors in the Formation of the Entrepreneurial Elite in South Korea." Asian Survey 16 (1976): 465-77.

Kim, Young C., and Abraham Halpern. The Future of the Korean Peninsula. New York: Praeger, 1977.

Kim, Young-Woo. "Evaluation of Korean Economic Growth in the 1960's." In Performance and Perspectives of the Korean Economy, edited by Kim Young-Woo. Tokyo: Institute of the Developing Economies, 1976.

Kuo, Eddie C. Y. "Multilingualism and Mass Media Communications in Singapore." Asian Survey 18 (1978): 1067-83.

Lee Soo Ann. Industrialization in Singapore. Victoria, Australia: Longman, 1973.

_____. Singapore Goes Transnational. Singapore: Eastern Universities Press, 1977.

_____. "The Economic System." In Singapore: Society in Transition, edited by Riaz Hassan. Kuala Lampur: Oxford University Press, 1976.

Lee, T. H. The Communist Organization in Singapore: Its Techniques of Manpower Mobilization and Management. Singapore: Institute of Southeast Asian Studies, 1976.

Lim Guek Poh. "Factory Girls in Jurong: An Ethnographic Study." Unpublished academic exercise, Department of Sociology, University of Singapore, 1974.

Lim, M. A. "The Hainanese of Singapore." Unpublished academic exercise, Department of Social Studies, University of Singapore, 1958.

Lofchie, Michael, and Carl Rosberg. "The Political Status of African Trade Unions." In The Role of Labor in African Nation-Building, edited by Willard Beling. New York: Praeger, 1968.

Low Nguan Kiang. "Nepotism in Industries: A Comparative Study of Sixty Chinese Modern and Traditional Industrial Enterprises." Unpublished academic exercise, Department of Sociology, University of Singapore, 1973.

Lynd, G. E. The Politics of African Trade Unionism. New York: Praeger, 1968.

McBeath, Gerald. "Taiwan in 1977: Holding the Reins." Asian Survey 18 (1978): 17-28.

McClelland, David. The Achieving Society. New York: Free Press, 1961.

McDiarmid, Orville. Unskilled Labor for Development. Baltimore: Johns Hopkins University Press, 1977.

Mak Lau-Fong. "The Sociology of Secret Societies." Review of Southeast Asian Studies 4 (1974): 1-2.

Malloy, James M. "Authoritarianism and Corporatism in Latin America: The Modal Pattern." In Authoritarianism and Corporatism in Latin America, edited by James Malloy. Pittsburgh: University of Pittsburgh Press, 1977.

Marshall, T. H. Class, Citizenship and Social Development. Garden City, N.Y.: Doubleday, 1964.

Merton, Robert K. "Social Structure and Anomie." In Social Theory and Social Structure, edited by Robert K. Merton. Glencoe, Ill.: Free Press, 1957.

Montagna, Paul. Occupations and Society: Toward a Sociology of the Labor Market. New York: Wiley, 1977.

Moore, Wilbert. Social Change. Englewood Cliffs, N.J.: Prentice-Hall, 1963.

_____. Industrialization and Labor: Social Aspects of Economic Development. Ithaca, N.Y.: Cornell University, 1951.

_____. The Impact of Industry. Englewood Cliffs, N.J.: Prentice-Hall, 1965.

Morris, Morris David. "Labor Relations: Developing Countries." In Comparative Perspectives on Industrial Society, edited by William Faunce and William Form, pp. 210-21. Boston: Little, Brown, 1969.

Nair, C. V. Devan. Socialism That Works . . . The Singapore Way. Singapore: Federal Publications, 1976.

Ngiam Tong Dow. "Taming the Singapore Job Hopper." Trends, NYLTI Journal, May 1977.

O'Donnell, Guillermo. "Corporatism and the Question of the State." In Authoritarianism and Corporatism in Latin America, edited by James Malloy. Pittsburgh: University of Pittsburgh Press, 1977.

Ooi Jin-Bee. "Singapore: The Balance-Sheet." In Modern Singapore, edited by Ooi Jin-Bee and Chiang Hai Ding. Singapore: University of Singapore, 1969.

Oshima, Harry. "Growth and Unemployment in Singapore." Malayan Economic Review 12 (1967): 32–58.

Pang Eng Fong. "Growth, Inequality and Race in Singapore." International Labour Review 111 (1975): 15–28.

Pang Eng Fong, and Linda Lim. The Electronics Industry in Singapore. Singapore: Chopmen Enterprises, 1977.

Pang Eng Fong, and Thelma Kay. "Change and Continuity in Singapore's Industrial Relations System." Department of Sociology, University of Singapore, Working Papers, no. 35 (1974).

Pang Eng Fong, and Tan Chwee Huat. "Foreign Investment, Unions, and the Government in Singapore." Asia Research Bulletin 2 (1972).

Parsons, Talcott. "Evolutionary Universals in Society." American Sociological Review 29 (1964): 339–57.

Parsons, Talcott, and Edward Shils, eds. Toward a General Theory of Action. New York: Harper & Row, 1951.

Pasara, Luis, and Jorge Santistevan. "Industrial Communities and Trade Unions in Peru: A Preliminary Analysis." International Labour Review 108 (1973): 2–3.

Pena, Felix. "Multinational Enterprises and North–South Relations." In Beyond Dependency, edited by Guy Erb and Valeriana Kallab. Washington, D.C.: Overseas Development Council, 1975.

Polanyi, Karl. The Great Transformation. Boston: Beacon Press, 1944.

Portes, Alejandro. "The Factorial Structure of Modernity." American Journal of Sociology 79 (July 1973): 15–44.

Price and Waterhouse. Singapore as an International Financial Centre. Singapore: Price and Waterhouse, 1976.

Przeworski, Adam. "Institutionalization of Voting Patterns, or Is Mobilization the Source of Decay?" The American Political Science Review 69 (March 1975): 49–67.

Purcell, Victor. The Chinese in Southeast Asia. London: Oxford University Press, 1951.

Rees, Albert. The Economics of Trade Unions. Chicago: University Press, 1977.

Ross, Arthur, and Paul Hartman. Changing Patterns of Industrial Conflict. New York: Wiley, 1960.

Schoultz, Lars. "The Socio-economic Determinants of Popular-Authoritarian Electoral Behavior: The Case of Peron." American Political Science Review 71 (1977).

Scoville, James. "Determinants of the Structure of the Labor Movements." In The International Labor Movement in Transition, edited by Adolf Sturmthal and James Scoville. Urbana: University of Illinois Press, 1973.

Seah Chee Meow. Community Centers: Their Political Involvement. Singapore: University of Singapore Press, 1973.

Seashore, Stanley. Group Cohesiveness in the Industrial Work Group. Ann Arbor: Survey Research Center, University of Michigan, 1954.

Seminar delegates. "Collective Bargaining and Labour Arbitration in Singapore." In Collective Bargaining and Labour Arbitration in the ASEAN Region. Bangkok: Friedrich-Ebert-Stiptung, 1977.

Shankman, Paul. "Growth, Multinational Corporations, and the Brazilian State." In Ethno-nationalism, Multinational Corporations, and the Modern State, edited by Ronald Grant and E. Spencer Wellhofer. Denver, Colo.: University of Denver, 1979.

Sharma, B. R. "The Indian Industrial Worker." International Journal of Comparative Sociology 10 (1969).

Shaw, K. E., Peter Chen, S. Y. Lee, and George Thomson. Elites and National Development in Singapore. Tokyo: Institute of Developing Economies, 1977.

Shils, Edward, and Morris Janowitz. "Cohesion and Disintegration in the Wehrmacht in World War II." The Public Opinion Quarterly 12 (Summer 1948): 280-315.

Singapore, Department of Statistics. Report on the Census of Services. Singapore: Government Printer, 1974.

Singapore International Chamber of Commerce. Investor's Guide. Singapore, 1976.

Singapore, Republic of. Commission of Inquiry into the Construction Capacity of Singapore, Final Report. Singapore: Government Printer, 1962.

Smelser, Neil. The Sociology of Economic Life. Englewood Cliffs, N.J.: Prentice-Hall, 1976.

Solomon, Lewis. Multinational Corporations and the Emerging World Order. Port Washington, N.Y.: Kennikat Press, 1978.

Snow, Robert. "Southeast Asia in the World System: Origins and Extent of Export Oriented Industrialization in the ASEAN Countries." Paper presented at 1980 Annual Meeting of the Association for Asian Studies, March 21-23, 1980. Washington, D.C.

Sturmthal, Adolf. "Unions in Developing Countries." In Comparative Labor Movements, edited by Adolf Sturmthal, pp. 138-50. Belmont, Calif.: Wadsworth, 1972.

_____. "Industrial Relations Strategies." In The International Labor Movement in Transition, edited by Adolf Sturmthal and James Scoville. Urbana, Ill.: University of Illinois, 1973.

Sufrin, Sidney. Unions in Emerging Societies. Syracuse, N.Y.: Syracuse University Press, 1964.

Suh, Sang-Chul. "External Economic Cooperation." In Performance and Perspectives of the Korean Economy, edited by Kim Young-Woo. Tokyo: Institute of Developing Economies, 1976.

_____. Growth and Structural Changes in the Korean Economy: 1910-1940. Cambridge, Mass.: Harvard University Press, 1978.

Suyama, Taku. "Pang Societies and Economy of Chinese Immigrants in Southeast Asia." In Papers on Malayan History, edited by K. Tregonning. Singapore, 1962.

Tae, Wan-Son. Development of the Korean Economy. Seoul: Samhwa Publishing Co., 1972.

Tan Chuan Lye. "Employment Practices of Selected Foreign Electronics Firms in Singapore." Unpublished academic exercise, Department of Sociology, University of Singapore, 1976.

Tan Chwee Huat. "The Public Enterprise as a Development Strategy: The Case of Singapore." Annals of Public and Co-operative Economy, January-March 1975.

Tan Ern Ser. "A Re-Appraisal of Singapore's Development." Unpublished academic exercise, Department of Sociology, University of Singapore, 1979.

Tan, I. T. "Business-Government Relations in Southeast Asia." Unpublished doctoral dissertation, Graduate School of Business Administration, New York University, 1972.

Tan Jin Lee, Winifred. "Chinese Kinship under Change in Singapore." Unpublished academic exercise, Department of Sociology, University of Singapore, 1976.

Tangri, Shanti. "Urbanization, Political Stability, and Economic Growth." In India's Urban Future, edited by Roy Turner. Berkeley: University of California Press, 1962.

Tannenbaum, Frank. A Philosophy of Labor. New York: Alfred Knopf, 1951.

Thompson, Thomas. "Taiwan's Ambiguous Destiny." Asian Survey 16 (1976): 611-19.

Tilly, Louise, and J. Scott. Women, Work, and Family. New York: Holt, Rinehart and Winston, 1978.

Turner, Louis. Multinational Companies and the Third-World. London: Allen Lane, 1973.

United Nations. A Proposed Industrialization Programme for the State of Singapore. U.N. Commission for Technical Assistance, Department of Economic and Social Affairs, 1961.

United Nations, Department of Economic and Social Affairs. Multinational Corporations in World Development. New York: Praeger, 1974.

U.S. Department of Health, Education, and Welfare. Work in America. Cambridge, Mass.: MIT Press, 1973.

Vernon, Raymond. Sovereignty at Bay. New York: Basic Books, 1971.

Waterman, Peter. "Workers in the Third World." Monthly Review 29 (1977).

Weber, Max. The Theory of Social and Economic Organization, Edited by Talcott Parsons. New York: Oxford University Press, 1947.

Wilensky, Harold, and Charles Lebeaux. Industrial Society and Social Welfare. New York: Russell Sage Foundation, 1958.

Wilson, Joan. The Singapore Rubber Market. Singapore: Eastern Universities Press, 1958.

Wong, Aline. "Women as a Minority Group." In Singapore: Society in Transition, edited by Riaz Hassan. Kuala Lampur: Oxford University Press, 1976.

Wong Saik Chin, and Peter S. J. Chen. The Impact of Community Centres on Social Development in Singapore. Bangkok: Clearing House for Social Development in Asia, 1977.

Yeh, Stephen H. K. Marriage and Family in a Developing Society. Singapore: Donald Moore Press, n.d.

Yong, C. F. "A Preliminary Study of Chinese Leadership in Singapore: 1900-1941." Journal of Southeast Asian History 9 (1968).

Yong Hon Loon. "The Practice of Nepotism: A Study of Sixty Chinese Commercial Firms in Singapore." Unpublished academic exercise, Department of Sociology, University of Singapore, 1973.

Yoshihara, Kunio. Foreign Investment and Domestic Response. Singapore: Eastern Universities Press, 1976.

NEWSPAPERS AND MAGAZINES

Asian Business and Industry. Singapore.

Asian Wall Street Journal. Hong Kong.

Business Times. Singapore (The Straits Times).

Far Eastern Economic Review. Hong Kong.

Labour News. Singapore (PIEU and SILO).

Singapore Economic Bulletin. Singapore.

The Singapore Straits Times. Singapore.

Sunday Nation. Singapore.

Sunday Times. Singapore (The Straits Times).

Wall Street Journal. New York.

INDEX

ABOUT THE AUTHOR

FREDERIC C. DEYO is Assistant Professor of Sociology at the State University of New York at Brockport. He was Lecturer in Sociology at the University of Singapore during the period 1974-78.

Dr. Deyo has published a number of articles on Asian industry and economic life which have appeared in the Journal of Asian Studies, the Journal of Management Studies, Human Organization, and the United Nations Economic Bulletin for Asia and the Pacific.

Dr. Deyo holds a B.A. from Yale University, an M.A. from the University of California at Berkeley, and a Ph.D. from the University of Chicago.